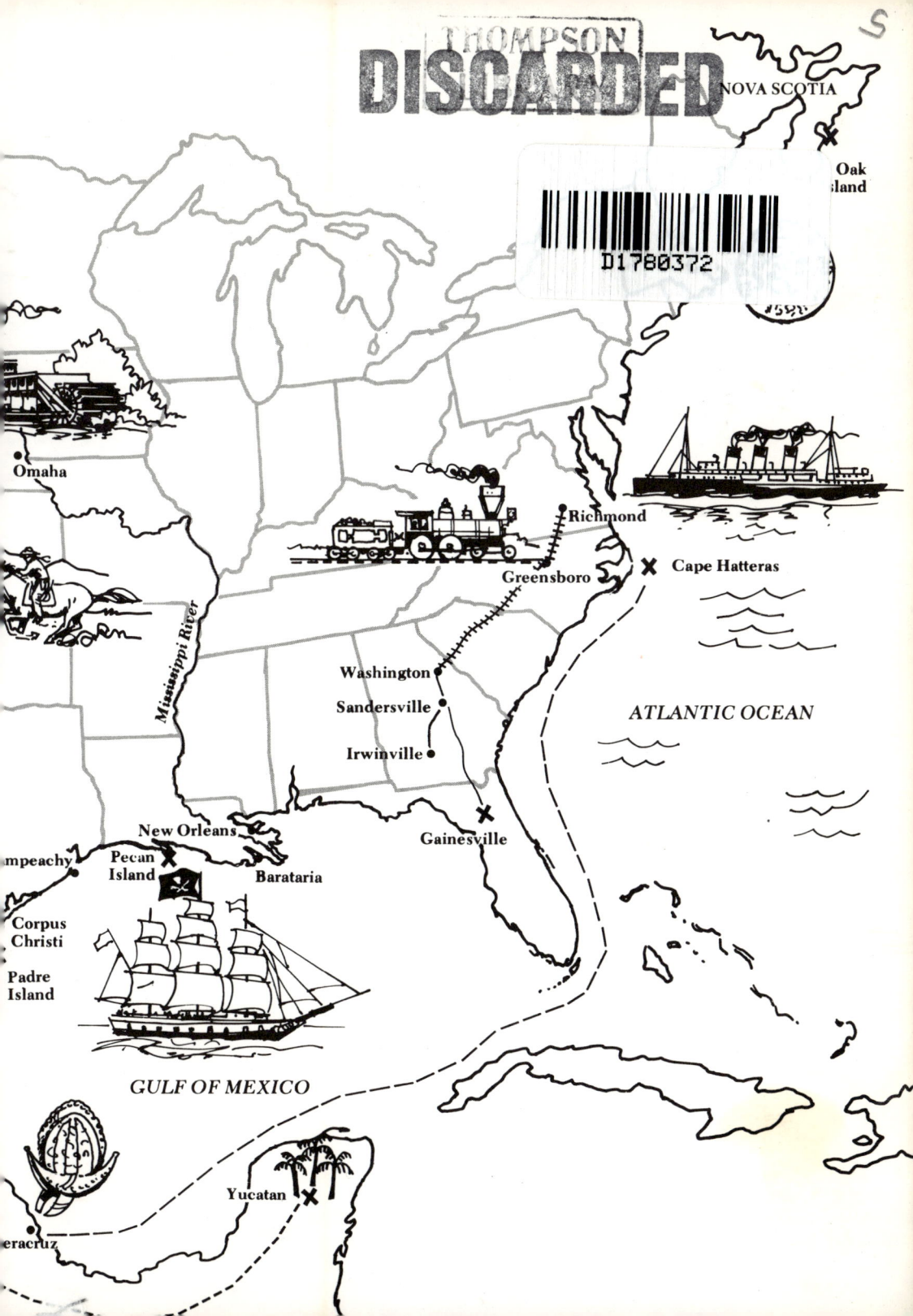

Lost Treasures of America
Searching Out Hidden Riches

LOST TREASURES OF AMERICA

Searching Out Hidden Riches

Arnold Madison

Illustrated by Dick Wahl

RAND McNALLY & COMPANY
Chicago　　New York　　San Francisco

For David Lee Drotar
—a gem of a writer and a treasured friend.

Library of Congress Cataloging in Publication Data
Madison, Arnold.
    Lost treasures of America.

    Includes index.
    SUMMARY: Describes the searches for lost treasures such as the White Sands Missile Base treasure whose existence is based on historical evidence.
    1. Treasure-trove—United States—Juvenile literature. (1. Buried treasure) I. Title.
E 179.M177   973   77-23918
ISBN 0-528-82153-9
ISBN 0-528-80035-3 lib. bdg.

Jacket illustration by Mike Mariano

Copyright © 1977 by Rand McNally & Company
All rights reserved
Printed in the United States of America
by Rand McNally & Company
First printing, 1977

Contents

1. Treasure Found, Treasure Lost — 13
2. Montezuma's Treasure — 19
3. Oak Island: The Money Pit — 31
4. The White Sands Missile Base Treasure — 45
5. Jean Lafitte's Booty — 59
6. The Burial Chamber of Kamehameha — 71
7. Treasure Train: The Confederate Papers — 79
8. Arizona's Lost Dutchman Mine — 87
9. The Treasure of the *Merida* — 101
10. Jesse James: His Cache — 109

Dig Deeper! — 121

Index — 123

1

Treasure Found, Treasure Lost

> *In an instant, a treasure of incalculable value lay gleaming before us. As the rays of the lanterns fell within the pit, there flashed upward a glow and a glare, from a confused heap of gold and of jewels, that absolutely dazzled our eyes.*
>
> Edgar Allan Poe

Lurking within all of us is the urge to be a treasure hunter. Let someone say, "I heard a story that there's supposed to be buried treasure around here somewhere," and the room suddenly gets quiet as everyone leans closer. In each listener's mind is a glimmer of hope that he or she will be the individual to find that fortune.

George Banks of Lewiston, Idaho, is such a person. He had embarked upon the hobby of treasure hunting modestly, searching for lost valuables with a metal detector. Scouring parks and fairgrounds, he unearthed lost coins, rings, and watches. One day a friend described a ghost town in northwestern Washington State. Banks decided to try his luck there. At first glance, nothing about the site indicated that here he would find a treasure far beyond anything he had dreamed.

"There wasn't much standing that would reveal the presence of an old town," he later told an interviewer.

A local resident, however, had told Banks that the ghost town once had a race track which, in the middle and late eighteen hundreds, attracted many horse fans. Pushing through the tall weeds and bushes, Banks located an area which seemed to be the old track. During the next few hours, his detector alerted him to various bits of metal. Surprisingly, most were modern coins which indicated the place had been used often by campers and backpackers.

"I was kind of disappointed at first, but I decided to continue working anyway," Banks said.

Soon his detector buzzed again. He dug down a few inches and pulled out an odd-looking coin about the size of today's quarter. One face showed the date, 1855, and the worth, twenty dollars. Also, the words "California Gold" were stamped on the coin. Knowing gold pieces are valuable, he carefully pocketed his find.

Through later research and consultations with gold and coin experts, Banks learned his coin's history. As early as 1848, the United States Government allowed private companies to mint gold coins. This was particularly important in California where money was scarce due to the rapid growth of the territory. The piece Banks found had been issued in December, 1855, by a Sacramento, California, firm. More exciting was the fact that today there are only two such coins in existence. One is owned by the Ford Foundation and the other is in the Smithsonian Institution. George Banks' twenty dollar gold piece is worth approximately $300,000.

Banks was lucky. But it was the type of luck successful treasure hunters have learned to develop. Banks had taken the time to become an expert with his metal detector. He researched his site by interviewing people who lived near the ghost town. And he didn't give up when his prospects appeared slim. Two other treasure hunters had the same kind of "luck" as George Banks.

Sam Corbino and Jess Pursell of Omaha, Nebraska, had heard stories about a paddle-wheeler which departed St. Louis in the late 1860s but never reached its destination. The *Bertrand* carried a cargo and passengers for the Fort Bend, Montana, gold fields. About twenty-five miles north of Omaha, the boat struck a submerged object and sank to the bottom of the Missouri River. Fortunately all forty crew members and passengers were rescued, but the ship and its cargo were never salvaged.

The first step in finding the treasure was to be certain that this was not another false treasure tale. Corbino and Pursell investigated the records of the old steamboat company. They tracked down newspaper articles about the wreck which contained interviews with the survivors. Other treasure hunters had done this too. But so far no one had found the remains of the *Bertrand*. Though anxious to begin the actual hunt, the two men continued their painstaking research. They met and talked with people who had lived on the river for many years. Then, on an old map of the region, they discovered a fact that others had missed.

Over the years the Missouri River had rerouted itself. So

while "unlucky" treasure hunters searched today's river bottom, Pursell and Corbino located the old riverbed about a quarter mile from the present Missouri River. The rotting hull of the 161-foot boat lay under thirty-five feet of soggy sand and shale mud. But it is the *Bertrand*'s 250-ton cargo which will repay Corbino and Pursell for their years of careful preparation and searching. Headed for the stores of Fort Bend were crates of jarred pickles, catsup, and vegetables along with 4,091 bottles of whiskey and bitters. Archaeologists estimate the bottles and jars are worth between twenty-five dollars and two hundred dollars each. The total value of the find is conservatively placed at $150,000.

Thousands of treasures such as the gold coin and the steamboat are scattered throughout America. Even more plentiful are phony stories about missing fortunes. If lost treasures excite you, this book may start you off in the right direction. All the incidents described in *Lost Treasures of America* are based on historical evidence. Yet these same riches have never been found even though many people have searched. Possibly you will be the one to unearth the single missing clue which will lead to their locations.

2

Montezuma's Treasure

> *O cursed lust for gold, to what dost thou not drive the hearts of men!*
>
> Virgil

In the year 1519, the Aztec civilization had reached its finest hour. The capital, Tenochtitlán, lay where the present-day Mexico City is located. The city was built on a lake with several large causeways connecting the temples, lush gardens, and red adobe buildings to the shore. The Aztecs were concerned about their environment, so the sanitation system did not dump any pollutants into the lake. Engineers had also developed a series of aqueducts to bring fresh water to the people, and a network of dikes to control the salinity of the lake water.

During their growth process, all great civilizations throughout history have created paper and a method of writing. The Aztecs, too, had achieved this accomplishment and were even producing their own literature. Another use for their writings was messages to the surrounding tribes which the Aztecs had conquered years before. The communiques demanded annual tribute to be sent to Tenochtitlán. As a result, the royal treasury was filled with gleaming emeralds as large as a fist, as well as solid gold ornaments cast in the forms of alligators, monkeys, and jaguars. Silver and gold plates as big around as wagon wheels were stored in the treasury vaults as were pieces of heavy armor made of silver and inlaid with precious gems.

Ruling over this kingdom was Moctezuma II or, as he is now called, Montezuma. Crowned in 1503, he had guided the Aztec nation well. These people might have become the most highly developed civilization in the Western Hemisphere had it not been for a decision made on an island in the Caribbean Sea. The Spanish governor of Hispaniola—the island which is now Haiti and the Dominican Republic—ordered Hernando Cortés to explore the Central American coast. The ships of the Spanish explorer landed at what is today the Mexican city of Veracruz, and Cortés and his conquistadores began their march inland.

At first the Aztecs had no inkling that this day in 1519 was to mark the beginning of their destruction. They believed, in fact, that they were being blessed by their gods. According to an ancient Aztec legend, *Quetzalcoatl,* or "plumed serpent," was a bearded white god who had arrived centuries before in a ship from the east. His craft was supposed to have landed exactly where Cortés anchored his ships. Quetzalcoatl had taught the Aztecs the ways of civilization. Then, after promising that he and his sons would return in a ship approaching from the sunrise, the god disappeared.

Therefore, when Montezuma heard about the column of troops and cavalrymen led by a bearded white man, he assumed Quetzalcoatl had come again. He dispatched a hundred porters who bore gifts to Cortés. The capes of tropical feathers, jewel-covered vases, and baskets of enormous pearls excited the Spaniard's greed. Immediately Cortés pushed on toward Tenochtitlán.

Montezuma personally welcomed Cortés and treated him as an honored guest. For four days the Spaniard played that role while his spies brought him reports that many of the Aztec buildings and temples were filled with rare treasures. On the fifth day he secretly made Montezuma his prisoner and instructed the Aztec ruler to issue whatever orders Cortés directed. Among the first was a command that all the Aztec treasures were to be collected and given to the Spaniards. The people obeyed, but reluctantly. Many silver and gold pieces were secretly held back and stored in hidden places. Nor did Montezuma relinquish the royal treasury to Cortés.

Cortés had to leave with a portion of his army to intercept an enemy force sent by the governor of Cuba to oust him. While he was away, his men attacked a peaceful festival in Tenochtitlán, slaughtering hundreds of Aztecs. The nation was horrified and sought revenge. A revolt broke out as Cortés was returning to the Aztec capital. He ordered Montezuma to speak to his people and stop the fighting. But the Aztecs would not listen to their ruler who they now knew to be little more than a slave of the Spanish invaders. When

Montezuma stepped before the unruly mob, he was struck with arrows and stones. He died June 30, 1520.

Before Cortés and his men could gather all the accumulated Aztec treasures, the Indians launched a frenzied attack and drove them from the city. Pursuing the Spaniards on the long march to the sea, the Indians continued the battle. Cortés lost a third of his men before reaching the safety of his fleet. Even more distressing to the adventurer was the fact that he had to leave behind many of the treasures he had so desperately wanted.

Meanwhile, the Aztec war chief, Cuitlahuac, had taken control of the government in Tenochtitlán. Realizing the Spaniards would return one day, he decided to remove the vast royal treasury to a place where it would be safe. Royal bearers were loaded up with the gold and jewels and began the long trek which would take them to the secret storage place.

The Spanish eventually raised a new army and fought their way into the Aztec capital. But the royal treasury was beyond their grasp. Only Cuitlahuac and the porters knew where the nation's wealth had been deposited. And the crafty war chief purposely saw that none of the bearers would reveal the secret. Those men who had not died during the fighting were selected as sacrifices to the Aztec war god. Now no waggling tongues could be tricked or bribed. But six months after he had ordered the royal valuables removed, Cuitlahuac himself fell victim to smallpox. The secret location of a cache of gold, estimated today to be worth at least ten million dollars, died with him.

There are several clues to this mystery to help a

searcher—some fanciful, some historically accurate.

The Aztecs might have borne the treasure south into the Yucatán jungle. If so, little hope remains for finding the gold. Whole cities have been swallowed by the fast-growing jungle foliage. Even when archaeologists know the location of an ancient temple, they may be only fifty feet away and fail to spot the vine-covered building.

Most accounts about Montezuma's treasure say the caravan went north. But how far north, and then in what direction? One version claims the party traveled 275 leagues north from Tenochtitlán and then headed west into high mountains. Since a league can vary from 2.4 to 4.6 miles, a person would have difficulty plotting the route!

Almost all reports agree that a cave was the hiding place. Legend also has it that the gold was hidden in or near a village of people friendly with or possibly related to the Aztecs.

If we follow those clues, the treasure might be in New Mexico. Aztec history states that their ancestors once came from the land that is now New Mexico. The Hopi Indians of nearby Arizona speak a language closely related to the Aztec tongue. And Pueblo Indian folklore says that Montezuma himself once visited Pecos which was south of modern-day Santa Fe.

The Aztec porters could have been ordered to a friendly Pueblo village. Their route would have then followed the Rio Grande so they would be near a water supply. There is another reasonable connection between the Pueblo Indians and the Aztec gold. The Pueblos had a special storage place for valuables called a *kiva*. A kiva was a chamber, at least partially underground, designed for religious and ceremonial purposes. The Aztecs would have considered a kiva the perfect location for the royal treasury, because they knew the Pueblo people believed kivas were protected by their gods. No thief would risk angering the gods by committing the sacrilege of looting a kiva. The Aztec gold would be safe in these dark, subterranean rooms.

But what about the numerous reports which state that a cave was the hiding place? The Aztec language had no word for kiva because all their religious temples were built on the tops of pyramids. So their use of the word for cave might be the closest in the Aztec tongue to describe a kiva.

The valley of the Rio Grande contains the authenticated ruins of more than thirty unexcavated pueblos. Many more may have existed and now be lost, eradicated by nature or man. Most of the known pueblos were inhabited at the time the Aztecs hid their royal treasury. Within the next hundred years, however, the Pueblo Indians were destroyed by war and disease. The secret of the exact kivas containing the Aztec wealth may have vanished with them.

New Mexico figures into another tale concerning the Aztec treasure. The *Weekly New Mexican* of July 14, 1876, reported that a young Mexican man had arrived in Taos and was searching for Montezuma's gold. Supposedly he climbed Taos Peak along with some of the townspeople. At one point he left the main group, scrambled up a high cliff, and vanished from view. In a little while he reappeared at the cliff's edge, calling to the people below. He had discovered a large cave filled with gold and lighted by the glow of many jewels. But, alas, before he could say anything more, a strong wind came up and blew him off the cliff!

This is the sort of treasure story a searcher should take very lightly. Newspapers at that time did not have staffs of reporters and therefore depended upon local people to feed them news items. Small newspapers today still use this method. The truth of this report is indeed in doubt when we learn that apparently no one ever climbed the cliff and hunted for the fabulous cavern of gems and gold.

But there is a more recent incident in which an entire town searched for the cave containing Montezuma's wealth. This town is not located in New Mexico, but in Utah.

One day in the summer of 1917, a prospector arrived at Oscar Robinson's ranch in Kanab, Utah. His name was Freddy Crystal, and he was seeking a rich person to grubstake his search for the Aztec gold. Crystal had an old Mexican newspaper clipping which showed a printed block of Aztec petroglyphs, or picture signs, carved into rock. He claimed he had found similar symbols in Johnson Canyon about thirty miles from Kanab. Somehow he convinced Robinson to finance an expedition to locate Montezuma's riches.

For the next two years Freddy Crystal clambered over the rocks and crevices of Johnson Canyon, seeking the cave. And then, in 1919, Crystal left one day and did not return.

Some people in Kanab thought perhaps he had died in a fall somewhere in the canyon. Others smiled knowingly and said that Crystal had found the treasure he really wanted— Oscar Robinson's money. One of the few persons who still believed that Crystal had been right about the Aztec treasure was Robinson.

Four years later Freddy Crystal again knocked on Robinson's door. He explained his absence by saying he had been to Mexico and, even more startling, had visited an old monastery there. In the monastery's records he had discovered a map over 400 years old. The map had been drawn on maguey plant paper which was the type of paper the Aztecs used. Crystal had not been allowed to take the actual map with him, but he did manage to make a copy.

The map was crude but depicted what appeared to be a large canyon from which four smaller draws branched off. Seven mountains ringed the canyon. Even though Crystal could not remember anything in Johnson Canyon resembling that arrangement, he requested more money from Robinson. The search was renewed.

At first no such site could be found. Then one day Crystal and a few ranch hands tried a different tack. They approached Johnson Canyon from the south. As they neared Sheep Mountain, Crystal spotted the seven mountains and the four draws leading off the main canyon. When they reached what the map showed as the north mountain, they found rough steps which were also indicated on the map. Holes the size of a human foot had been carved into the stone, leading up the volcanic rock incline. The men continued on foot until they found themselves against the perpendicular face of White Mountain. Further movement was impossible. Had the hand-hewn steps led only to a dead end?

Studying the wall, Crystal detected something different about one portion. Part of the mountain face was sand and not stone. The men dug away at the sand, and after a few hours they realized that they were digging at the mouth of a cave packed full of sand.

Keeping their discovery a secret, the men worked each

day for the next week until they had unearthed a sixty-foot tunnel. But now the diggers were faced with another barrier —blocks of blue limestone. The wall was five yards long and had obviously been constructed to seal off whatever was behind. Even more puzzling were the blocks themselves. The rough blocks had been crudely cut and cemented together with marsh clay which had bits of wire grass embedded in it. The men knew that blue limestone could be found some miles away, but there was no marsh clay and wire grass for miles. Then someone recalled hearing stories that there had been marshes in that section of Utah hundreds of years before that time.

Fired with renewed enthusiasm, Crystal and the ranch hands continued their excavation. The news of their discovery, however, had reached the townspeople. Within days the entire town's population was digging to remove the stone blockade. For three months the main goal of every citizen in Kanab, Utah, was Montezuma's treasure.

When the tunnel had been extended 160 feet into White Mountain, the workers discovered several natural chambers with tunnels branching off each of them. Someone must have lived in these rooms because there were charcoal ashes plus deer and rabbit bones. But where was the treasure?

Further exploration and digging unearthed nothing more. Interest began to lag, and many of the people returned to their regular life. Freddy Crystal and a few inveterate searchers continued digging until, discouraged, they too gave up. Packing his belongings, Freddy Crystal left Kanab for the last time and returned to Mexico.

Over the years, new treasure hunters have worked the

site, but with the same results. Bill Jons of Kanab obtained a mineral lease on the area in 1967. Using metal detectors, Jons claimed to have located four hidden chambers which previous searchers had not touched. But he has not found any treasure to this day.

As improbable as Crystal's account of how he found the map may be, the sketch did lead him to this strange cave. Even if Montezuma's treasury is not inside White Mountain, the tunnel is intriguing. Why would people quarry the limestone blocks and fill the cave mouth with sand unless they were trying to hide something? Could the cave be a blind meant to trick treasure hunters? Yet that mysterious treasure still eludes everyone.

Today railroad yards and slums cover the area where the Aztec civilization died. In a museum in Vienna, Austria, you can see the magnificent quetzal plume headdress which Montezuma gave to Cortés when he still thought the Spaniard was a friend of the Aztecs. But where is Montezuma's royal treasury?

Wherever the Aztec gold may be—in a Pueblo kiva or inside a Utah mountain—ten million dollars worth of gold and gems still awaits some lucky treasure hunter as it has for over 450 years.

3

Oak Island: The Money Pit

...what wealth lies hid in the secret caves of earth.

Margaret Fuller

An island off the coast of Nova Scotia has generated such tremendous excitement in the United States and Canada that treasure hunters have been digging there for over 180 years. And yet after all this time there are still basic questions left unanswered. For instance, nobody knows what is there, who buried whatever may be there, or even if anything *is* there. Yet, armed with only the scantiest of information, men have invested millions of dollars in the search.

The story started simply enough. In the summer of 1795, sixteen-year-old Daniel McGinnis was canoeing in Mahone Bay. After about four miles he decided to explore Oak Island which was named for its heavy growth of red oak trees. The day was bright and warm so he ignored the local tales that Oak Island was haunted. As he paddled into a crescent-shaped cove, he spotted a large boulder near the shore. A heavy ringbolt had been fastened into the half-submerged rock. Daniel found this curious because the small island was uninhabited.

Following an old path, he hiked about the island until he came into a clearing which had an ancient oak tree in its center. Hanging from a branch approximately sixteen feet above the ground was an old ship's tackle block. The earth under the block had a strange depression about twelve feet across. Glancing around, Daniel noticed the site had been cleared some time before because new foliage almost covered the old oak stumps.

The clues added up to only one thing for Daniel, who had lived his whole life along this Nova Scotia coast. Pirates were frequent visitors to this region. One group of them must have buried a treasure on Oak Island.

He immediately paddled back to Chester, a small town on the eastern shore of Mahone Bay, and alerted two of his friends. The next day Daniel, Anthony Vaughan, and John Smith went to the island. When one boy climbed the gnarled oak and touched the tackle block, the device fell and shattered. Armed with picks and spades, the boys began digging directly underneath the branch which had held the old tackle block.

After removing most of the loose topsoil, they discovered a thirteen-foot circular shaft with walls of hard clay. When the hole was four feet deep, their shovels hit a layer of flagstones. Rocks of that type were not found on Oak Island, so the boys knew they must have been brought from another location. At ten feet there was a platform of oak logs. The outside of the logs had rotted, indicating that the wood had been buried for a long time. At the twenty-foot level there was a second layer of logs, and another at thirty feet.

Obviously the excavation was not going to be a matter of simply digging up a buried chest of gold. The boys decided to get help. Twenty-one-year-old John Smith purchased the discovery area, and he and Daniel McGinnis settled on the island. They were warned by local inhabitants not to stay there at night. A woman reported that her mother, one of the original settlers of the region, once had seen strange lights and fires there. Two men had rowed out to the island to investigate. They never returned. The reputation of Oak Island complicated the boys' task of raising enough money for an intensive search of the pit.

Finally, nine years later, the three original hunters had formed a syndicate with three other men. Work was begun in 1804 on what would come to be called the "money pit." More odd finds were uncovered as the shaft went deeper and deeper. At the thirty-foot point, the diggers found charcoal, and at forty feet another layer of logs which were covered with putty. Farther down more charcoal, another platform, and coconut fiber. One man reported that the coconut fiber was brought up by the bushel.

And then, at the ninety-foot depth, the searchers encountered what might have been an important clue. A flat stone about three feet long and one foot wide lay in the dirt. Although the sides were rough with bits of cement sticking to them, the top and bottom surfaces were smooth. There appeared to be letters and symbols carved into one surface.

The letters, if that's what they were, seemed too roughly cut for any of the searchers to interpret. But the men believed that they were nearing the treasure and pressed on enthusiastically. In their intense excitement, they failed to attach any importance to the fact that the earth was becoming increasingly soft and moist. Soon they were bringing up buckets of water more often than containers of earth. At the ninety-eight-foot mark, one man jabbed an iron bar into the soil and struck something hard. He thought the substance was another layer of wood, but others thought it might be a chest.

Darkness made further work impossible, so the men stopped and sat about the fire, discussing how the treasure would be shared among them. When they returned the next morning, they found that water had flooded the pit to the thirty-three-foot level. When the team tried to bale the water out, it flowed in again from some unknown source.

Another plan was formulated. They would dig a second shaft alongside the original and drain the important hole. When the group had dug down 110 feet, they tunneled sideways into the main shaft. Water gushed into the second pit so quickly the men almost drowned before they reached the safety of the surface. The second pit filled to the same thirty-three-foot level. Amazingly, these men did not detect an important clue about the water, a clue which would have to wait for another expedition. The syndicate's finances were depleted, and their excavations had to be halted.

This was the end of the first organized effort to locate the unknown treasure, but merely the beginning of the Oak

Island story, a most amazing treasure tale.

A new excavation company was organized in 1845 with only one of the original three men as a member—Anthony Vaughan. Over the years the pit had collapsed, but the men soon located the site and began digging. Once they had reached a depth of eighty-six feet, however, they encountered flooding which brought the water again to the thirty-three-foot level.

When efforts to drain the pit failed, they hit upon another means to learn what was hidden deep in the shaft. A platform was constructed above the pit and a primitive type of drill called a pod auger was set up. Several borings were made to the depth of 106 feet, producing important findings.

At ninety-eight feet, the auger pierced the solid surface the previous expedition had hit with the iron bar. This was a layer of spruce. But right below that, the drill point went through four inches of oak and immediately into twenty-two inches of metal in pieces, and then into eight more inches of oak and another twenty-two inches of metal, and then through four inches of oak!

The workers concluded that there were two chests set upon one another. The lid of each oaken chest was four inches thick, they supposed. Under these chests was another spruce platform and, below that, seven feet of clay with seemingly nothing lodged in it. With these observations as encouragement, the company decided to sink still another shaft in order to tunnel into the main pit at the level where the "chests" were located. This pit, the third to be dug since 1795, went down 109 feet through hard clay. Although this shaft was only ten feet from the main pit, the digging crews did not strike water. When they dug a connecting tunnel, however, water poured into the new shaft, quickly flooding it. Though their efforts to drain either hole failed, the searchers had made an important discovery.

The water which filled the pit was seawater and even reacted to the tidal ebb and flow. If the liquid had been natural seepage, *each* of the shafts would have met water. But only the main pit was affected until the connecting tunnels were burrowed.

Could the people who first constructed the original shaft have built a tunnel to the sea in an effort to protect their treasure?

A search was conducted along the shore where Daniel McGinnis had first landed. The inlet was now called Smith's Cove in honor of John Smith. The men made an amazing discovery. Brownish fiber and eelgrass had been put down to cover five stone channels and keep them from being clogged with sand. These catchment channels, stretching 145 feet along the beach front, fed seawater into one big tunnel aimed at the money pit 500 feet away. The time and effort to construct this system would have been enormous. One engineer has estimated that it would have taken six months for nearly one hundred men to build the catchments, tunnels, and the pit.

But now the treasure seekers had to find a way to block the seawater from reaching the pit. A cofferdam was built to hold the sea back from the catchment channels. An extremely high tide wrecked the dam. The men next sank shafts in an effort to find the underground tunnel that carried the water to the pit. Again they failed. In one last desperate attempt, they dug another shaft and tunneled into the money pit at the 118-foot level. But the pit caved in and collapsed. With its funds gone, the second syndicate abandoned the search. But many more engineers, geologists, and treasure seekers were to arrive on Oak Island over the years.

In 1860 another company tried to defeat the water barrier and lost. An 1864 team also met defeat. Diggers in 1893 located what they thought was the flood tunnel and blocked it with dynamite, only to discover that water was entering the pit through another tunnel. The only find this team made occurred when a driller found a tiny fragment of parchment on a drill bit. The letters *ui, vi,* or *wi* appeared to have been written on the paper with ink and a quill pen. The syndicate had spent $100,000 for a shred of paper.

Franklin D. Roosevelt provided partial financial backing for a 1909 project which attacked the pit without success. Another effort was made by a New Jersey millionaire in 1936. Failure again.

And then, in the summer of 1965, the money pit exacted another price from those seeking to unravel its mysteries—life. A Canadian steelworker named Robert Restall had arrived in 1959 to locate the treasure.

"Shut off the water and you will find the treasure," Restall said.

On August 17, 1965, Restall, his son, and two other men were overcome by carbon monoxide fumes from a pump—and drowned in the hole they were digging.

Since 1967 a group of Canadian and American businessmen called the Triton Alliance has been at work on Oak Island with drills and excavators. So far the work on this latest project has cost more than half a million dollars.

What have the men gained for their $500,000?

Searchers have found pieces of iron and brass dated by experts to before 1850, a nail dated to 1750, and a heart-shaped stone. The problem now is that modern-day teams may be finding objects left behind by earlier treasure hunters rather than by the mysterious people who originally constructed the pit.

Triton workers did make one discovery which caught the attention of the Canadian and American news media. Having drilled a 212-foot shaft down the money pit—the deepest ever made on the island—the men lowered a television camera. The monitor screen on the surface showed what appeared to be three chests, a digging tool, and a scarred hand severed at the wrist. Photographs taken from the TV screen, however, were not as promising. They did show objects which did not seem of natural origin, but the images were so fuzzy that it was difficult to tell exactly what they were. To lower a person down the 212-foot shaft would be dangerous. To excavate to the 212-foot level would be extremely expensive.

And that's where the Oak Island mystery remains at the moment. After a period of over 180 years, the investment of four million dollars, and the cost of six lives, the questions are still unanswered. Who? What? Why?

The *why* should be the easiest, but then again possibly not. The first reaction as to why someone would construct a pit and protect whatever was there with an elaborate system of water tunnels is that something tremendously valuable must be hidden there. And placed there so that it could be retrieved at a future date. But that answer leads to another question. If the searchers are encountering so much difficulty unearthing the treasure, how were the people who placed it there going to recover their prize?

There are several possibilities. The people who constructed the tunnel system obviously had great engineering skill. They may have built another entrance to the pit. No search team has found such an entryway, but the workers cannot even locate the tunnels which are carrying the seawater to the pit. Another theory is that the tunnels originally had sea gates to control the flow of water. Therefore the original builders may have assumed that, when they returned, they would block the water and reclaim their treasure. Over the years, however, the chemical action of the salt water may have destroyed these gates.

One author has even theorized that the pit is a decoy and the real treasure lies buried somewhere else on the island. If that is true then the person who engineered the pit has to have been the world's greatest practical joker.

Some preposterous suggestions for the *who* and *what* of Oak Island have been offered.

The parchment fragment found in 1893 prompted some persons to say that chests containing the original, handwritten copies of Shakespeare's plays were buried there. As to how or why anyone would want to hide the manuscripts eludes those who favor this possibility.

Other people tell how the Inca Indians outfoxed Francisco Pizarro in the 1520s. When the Incas learned the Spaniards were looting Indian treasures, the natives of Tumbez, Peru, spirited away the valuables to be hidden until they might safely be returned. Hidden, say the supporters of this theory, on Oak Island. Again, the means or the reason for transporting treasures from the west coast of South America to the northeastern coast of North America are vague.

The collection of farfetched explanations includes one that states Norse sailors built the pit during their early voyages to North America. Those who accept this overlook the clues which point out that the clearing Daniel McGinnis discovered was not that old. Besides, what treasures would the Norsemen have wanted to hide here? Another group of individuals say that the pit contains the jewels of Marie Antoinette who had been executed two years before the pit was first discovered. They ignore the fact that her jewels were never lost.

Some believers claim there is a psychic clue as to who buried the mysterious treasure. In the late 1930s, the Adams family lived on Oak Island where they were employed as caretakers. One winter's day Peggy Adams ran to her mother, saying she had seen "many men wearing red coats and hats looking like firemen's helmets." Her mother accompanied the four-year-old girl to the site which was located between Smith's Cove and the money pit. But the only footprints Mrs. Adams found in the snow were those of Peggy's boots. The girl insisted that she was neither lying nor playing games, but the incident became no more than a family joke.

A few years later the Adamses visited the Citadel in Halifax which contains effigies of British soldiers. The life-size figures wear British uniforms of the period 1754–1783 which are red and have hats resembling firemen's helmets.

"Those are the men I saw," Peggy told her mother.

Had Peggy changed time dimensions and caught sight of British soldiers on a secret mission to bury a treasure? Some people believe so. But then there was a man who was certain the pit contained a full-scale model of the Great Pyramid of Egypt. The pyramid had been buried, he claimed, inverted and with a giant treasure under its apex! About the only supposition not offered so far is that beings from outer space were somehow responsible for the money pit.

The most accepted explanation of what might be hidden on Oak Island is the "pirate communal bank" theory. This speculation does seem to have some substantial evidence on its side. In 1965 a Spanish gold coin dated 1598 was found on the island. Some years earlier an underground pirate treasure bank had been discovered on Haiti. This treasure hoard, too, was protected by a water-flooding system similar to the Oak Island network of catchment channels and flood tunnels. As further proof, the people who favor this theory say that the Haitian pirate bank was marked by a heart-shaped stone like the one found by the Triton Alliance.

The presence of the coconut fibers in the first shaft is even more conclusive evidence that whoever had constructed the pit had come from the Caribbean Sea. Coconut fiber was once used as packing for ships' cargoes in that area of the world. So any boat with a precious cargo originating from a port in the Caribbean would probably have had a great deal of coconut fiber aboard. And one early searcher did say the workers brought up bushels of coconut fiber from the first shaft.

Did several pirates pool their ill-gotten gain and ship the wealth north for deposit in an underground bank? The Triton

Alliance hopes this may be the answer because then they might get back their investment.

One person jokingly said that "money pit" was the best possible name for the Oak Island digging—because so much investment money has been dumped into searching for the mysterious treasure. Without a doubt, the Oak Island treasure has been the object of the most costly treasure hunt in the history of man.

4

The White Sands Missile Base Treasure

*Bell, book and candle shall not drive me back,
When gold and silver becks me to come on.*

William Shakespeare

There is a treasure so vast that, if recent estimates are correct, it could well be the richest in the world. The quest for this hoard has created court cases involving the U.S. Department of Defense, the state of New Mexico, the U.S. Treasury Department, and one of the most famous lawyers in the United States. Also, as happens too often in many treasure hunting expeditions, a man shot and killed his partner when an argument erupted.

The site is a 500-foot hill named Victoria, or Victorio, Peak which is splattered with patches of mesquite, cactus, and numerous rock outcroppings. The peak is west of Alamogordo and east of Truth or Consequences, New Mexico, near the desolate San Andres Mountains. The region is now part of the federal government's White Sands Missile Base. It is the unhappy history of this ugly little hill, however, which is important to understanding exactly what treasures may be stashed there in Victoria Peak.

In 1759 the Spanish priest Padre La Rue arrived in Mexico with forty settlers. In addition to his prime responsibility of converting the Indians to Christianity, Padre La Rue had been asked by the Mexican authorities to uncover any available information about gold or other treasures. La Rue was successful in both tasks. A convert named Pacifico brought him to Victoria Peak which was then in Mexican territory. Pacifico led La Rue to the vertical shaft of an old Indian mine containing a rich vein of gold. The earthly temptation was too great for the priest.

Secretly he enlisted several members of his congregation to begin operating the mine. First they removed an enormous amount of ore which was then smelted into rough bricks. Each gold brick weighed between forty and seventy pounds. The bricks were later transported to a hiding place elsewhere on Victoria Peak. Week by week as the smelter purified and melted the ore, the cache grew, filling the main cave and then another room of the cavern.

The news that somewhere on Victoria Peak was a gold mine run by a priest eventually reached Mexican authorities. More importantly, they were told, the mine had already produced millions in gold. La Rue and his followers were arrested and questioned. None of them, though tortured, would disclose the secret location of the gold bricks. The Mexican officials ordered the men to be burned at the stake. Apparently La Rue and the other men went to their deaths without revealing the hiding place.

The rough, hostile area continued to breed violence. During the late 1870s and the early 1880s, Victorio, the last great Apache chief, led his band of 300 warriors in raids against El Paso and Ciudad Juárez. The Indians stored their loot in what is now New Mexico and, according to legend, in Victoria Peak. One account claims the mountain was originally named for the Apache leader, but over the years common usage has changed the name to Victoria. Reportedly included in the Indians' accumulated booty were La Rue's hidden gold blocks.

During the next fifty years, legends and stories grew and spread about the treasure of Victoria Peak. Numerous searches were conducted on the area, but without success. Then in 1937 a chiropodist from Hot Springs, New Mexico, was hunting deer in the hills. While scampering up Victoria Peak, "Doc" Milton Noss spotted an opening in the hillside. Upon further examination he discovered that the space was a cave which led to a shaft. Descending the vertical shaft, Noss found a large cavern filled with black bars.

The bars were stacked in piles and, as proved later, weighed about forty to seventy pounds each. When Noss scraped off the black coating, the glint of gold twinkled in the dim light. There were other more grisly occupants of the underground chamber. Noss reported seeing two skeletons chained to an iron ring between three wooden poles. In another section of the cave were the bones of a third person with red hair still on the skull.

Over the next two years Noss often visited the cavern.

At times his wife, Ova, accompanied him to the site, but Noss always went into the cavern alone. Mrs. Noss later told an *Albuquerque Tribune* reporter that " 'Doc' built a big fire down there once and we watched the mountain, hoping that escaping smoke would reveal other entrances."

When this failed, Noss resigned himself to always entering the cavern through the shaft. In addition to the gold bricks, Noss discovered other items: jewelry, old coins, Wells Fargo strongboxes and a silver napkin ring inscribed *"Talbot Hall, November 17, 1868."*

"Doc" Noss removed five gold bricks and brought them to the U.S. mint in Denver where an assay showed each was approximately sixty percent gold and forty percent copper. The value, Treasury agents told him, was $20.67 per ounce. Private citizens by law were not allowed to possess gold, so the mint held onto the bricks and gave Noss a receipt for $97,000. He quickly calculated the number of bars he had found up to this point and learned their total worth amounted to $2,656,000. And this was only a portion of the treasure. Other passages, blocked by rocks and debris, branched off the main chamber. He was certain more gold bricks were hidden in these tunnels.

For ten years Noss attempted to open the other passages. Unfortunately his skill with explosives was poor. Often the powder charge was too large or incorrectly placed, and with the blast the passage would be clogged full of fallen dirt and rocks. During this time Noss reportedly supported himself by selling bits of the jewelry and the nineteenth century relics on the black market.

Mrs. Noss claimed that "Doc" had shown her several of

the more exceptional relics he had found in the chamber. One was a seven-pound gold crown inlaid with 243 diamonds and a large ruby. The crown was inscribed with the date 1856. Noss explained to Ova that the crown might have been owned by Maximillian who had been emperor of Mexico between 1864 and 1867. When Maximillian realized that he would soon be deposed, he sent a large portion of his treasury and the crown jewels out of Mexico in 1866. Bandits attacked the treasure train while the caravan was en route to San Antonio. Noss figured the White Sands cavern had been used by bandits in the middle 1860s.

In 1946 Noss went to Arkansas, established legal residence, and divorced Ova. The charges he brought against his wife were that she had deserted him and could not be located. When Noss returned to New Mexico, however, he learned his prospecting permit had lapsed. Even worse was the fact that Ova had filed for the claims in her name. The Land Office did grant Noss a permit which allowed him to prospect passages on three sides of the cavern.

At different times since first discovering the shaft, Noss had attempted to form partnerships. Oddly, the syndicates were always disbanded. Whether Noss was too secretive about the gold he had already hidden, or whether the task of clearing the passages was too frustrating, he seemed incapable of working with another person. In 1949, however, he teamed up once again, this time with an oil and mining engineer named Charles Ryan. An agreement was signed which stated that Ryan would invest $27,000 as well as work with Noss to clear the passages. In return Ryan would receive fifty-one bars of gold.

The area around Victoria Peak was becoming crowded. Ova Noss and a son by a former marriage, Marvin Beckwith, were camped nearby in a trailer. "Doc" Noss and Charles Ryan were also living near the peak. Ryan had convinced Noss that trucking supplies into the camp was costing them valuable time. So the two men began to construct a simple landing strip. While this work was in progress, they arranged for pilot Curtis Noble to fly them additional supplies from Albuquerque.

By coincidence Beckwith was in Albuquerque and learned that Noble was flying to Victoria Peak. Beckwith paid Noble to allow him to be a passenger on the flight. The light plane was nearing Victoria Peak when it unexplainably went out of control and crashed. Noble died. Beckwith was severely injured. Noss drove to the accident scene and spoke briefly with Marvin Beckwith.

Later the *Associated Press* reported, "Apparently Beckwith told Noss something that caused alarm and was responsible for him going out late that same night, removing some of the gold from wherever he had previously cached it, and burying it again elsewhere."

Two days later "Doc" Milton Noss was found dead near his pickup truck. Charles Ryan surrendered voluntarily to the police. During his trial, Ryan testified that a fierce argument had erupted between them when he accused Noss of cheating him. "Doc" rushed to his truck to get a gun, but before he could fire, Ryan found his own gun and got off two shots. The jury acquitted Ryan of murder, stating that he had shot in self-defense.

At this time Ova Noss claimed all rights to the Victoria

Peak treasure. She continued the search. In 1955 the area became the Holloman Air Force Base Missile Testing Range (White Sands). Ova Noss was notified by base officials that neither she nor anyone else would be permitted in the vicinity of Victoria Peak. And that was the beginning of court actions by Ova and other individuals demanding to be allowed to search for the treasure. The air force steadfastly refused such permission—though there were rumors that both civilians and military personnel were carrying out secret missions.

Although the Defense Department is charged with the surveillance of the territory, the land is still owned by the state of New Mexico. When the state officials negotiated with the federal government for a lease on the region as a missile range, they insisted upon one important stipulation in the agreement. There were too many stories about lost gold mines and treasure hoards to be dismissed, so the state had a clause put into the contract retaining the mineral rights for itself. Though the move was a wise one, both state officials and members of the Department of Defense were to have problems stemming from this agreement.

In the fall of 1958 Capt. Leonard Fiege and three friends were deer hunting on the White Sands Missile Range. In a sworn affidavit later signed by the captain and his friend, Tom Berclett, Fiege described what happened that day.

The party had separated, and Fiege went down a canyon by himself. There he saw "this small hill and open caves." He climbed the hill and found a small cave fairly well hidden. The others had not arrived yet, so Fiege decided to do a little exploring. Entering the cave he came to a thirty-inch opening in one wall. He shone in his flashlight and saw that the opening led to a large shaft. Fiege crawled through on his stomach. The air was foul and the dust thick, so he sat down on what he thought was a dust-covered pile of rocks.

Fiege soon discovered the pile was not rocks but "smelted gold in bars about the size of a house brick." There were three such piles in plain view and a fourth partly covered by a collapsed wall of the cave. Two of the men were too large to squeeze through the opening, so only Tom Berclett reentered the shaft with Fiege. "Tom and I handled the gold and thought about taking some of it out but decided against it because we were not familiar with laws that governed the claiming of gold."

Fiege and Berclett decided to close off the entrance with rocks and dirt so the tunnel would appear to come to a dead end. Having thus protected their find, Fiege returned to the base where the judge advocate, Lt. Col. Sigmund I. Gasiewicz, instructed him to file a formal legal claim to the gold bars as treasure trove. Fiege and his friends had to wait almost three years for any action—three years filled with excuses. The most common one was that many unexploded 20 mm shells had landed on the White Sands Missile Range, burying themselves in the sand. These shells would be dangerous for anyone wandering through or digging in the area. Fiege kept urging the officials to reach a decision before other parties found the gold and either claimed the treasure or removed the bars illegally.

Finally, on August 5, 1961, Fiege and his friends were granted permission to return to the cave. They were accompanied by the commanding officer of the base, U.S. secret service agent Liburn Boggs, and fourteen military police. Whatever happened that day is obscured by the various versions of the story, though all participants do agree that the expedition was a failure.

One person claimed the thirty-inch opening led to an old iron mine; there was no gold. Another individual reported that Fiege was unable to find the cave entrance. Boggs said the captain did find the entrance, but the opening was completely clogged with dirt and rocks.

Angered by the ridicule, Fiege insisted he be given a lie detector test to prove he was telling the truth. On September 13, 1961, Fiege underwent the test which indicated his story that he had seen the gold bars was indeed true. Pressed by Fiege, the military officials agreed that he might explore Victoria Peak for two months. The permit specified that the search was "limited to the project area, travel allowed only on the entrance road, no cameras, guns or liquor permitted."

About this same time, officials of the state of New Mexico had been receiving reports that "unidentified military personnel as well as civilians both individually and in small groups" were conducting treasure hunts on Victoria Peak. A sum of $250,000 was appropriated for a survey of the area which hopefully would settle the question of whether or not a gold mine existed there. The Museum of New Mexico hired a Denver mining company to handle the job.

The Department of Defense granted permission for the mineral survey but stipulated that "The area to be explored is limited to the triangle within the three arroyos around Victoria Peak. There is to be no search for clues to valuables beyond this perimeter."

The Gaddis Mining Company investigated the limited area and found artifacts dating to the fourteenth century and some shell pieces from the missile tests—but no evidence of a mine. Their report definitely stated that La Rue's mine had not been located within the triangle. "If it had we would have found some evidence of gold ore, slag dumps, or tailings. Nor did the seismographic soundings disclose the existence of any large subterranean cavern. If a treasure was or is there it was brought from some other location and stored here by persons as yet unknown."

Had the base officials purposely limited the area of the search because they wanted to hide something? On October 28, 1961, sworn affidavits were presented to the Land Office testifying that a party visited Victoria Peak and were informed that four soldiers and four airmen were working the Noss claims. The Land Office checked with the base officials who said there was no such work being done at Victoria Peak. Less than a month later Maj. Gen. John G. Shinkle, the base commander, admitted to the Commissioner of Public Lands of New Mexico that operations were being conducted there as a joint effort between the Department of Defense and the Treasury Department.

Ova Noss, although she was not allowed into the Victoria Peak area, was keeping a watchful eye on her claims. She discovered that the work force on Victoria Peak was larger than the base officials claimed. Eight servicemen and about six military policemen were there with a jeep, a weapons carrier, and a large amount of shoring timber. Ova hired a lawyer and promptly brought suit for what she considered her rightful property.

Over the years other people have come to believe the Victoria Peak treasure belongs to them. Mr. F. Lee Bailey has been retained as the attorney for a group of fifty unidentified people. In June 1973 he contacted the Department of Defense, seeking permission to enter the Victoria Peak region.

"Give me just thirty minutes and a helicopter and I can lead the commanding general right to the treasure and show it to him."

Permission was denied.

Surprise agreement was granted in March 1977, however, but not to Bailey. "Operation Goldfinder" was allowed to enter the White Sands Missile Range and search Victoria Peak for one week only.

"The army's position is that there is no gold on this installation," stressed Maj. Kenneth Able. But years of refusing civilians' requests to search the area were over when the army decided to permit one all-out search in the hope that such an expedition would "put the legends to rest once and for all."

On March 21, 1977, one group of the six engaged in legal battles entered through Cottonwood Canyon. Mrs. Noss, "Doc"'s first wife, looked on as the search began. She admitted that although she was not contesting the search, she was in no way surrendering her rights to the treasure. The expedition members were warned by the military to be on the lookout for rattlesnakes and unexploded ordnance. Hopes were high, however, on that March day as they began to take radar soundings to determine if indeed there was a tunnel behind a boulder-clogged opening. Should a cavern have been discovered, excavation would have been facilitated through bulldozers and picks and shovels. The permit ran out on March 28, 1977—seven days later.

What did the group have to show for this rare opportunity to explore Victoria Peak?

Nothing.

Today there are numerous suits and countersuits in the courts. The legal proceedings may take years to untangle—if they can be settled at all. Once again civilians are not permitted to enter the White Sands Missile Base to learn whether or not there is a gold mine or a treasure cache. At least three people claim to have seen the gold bars, but at the moment no one can produce a bar as evidence. "Doc" Noss said he gave five bars to the Denver Mint, but Ova cannot find the receipt he was supposedly given. The paper was either lost or stolen. Ova maintains that she has requested permission to check through the mint's records, but the Treasury officials have not let her do this.

Is there really a 225-billion-dollar treasure somewhere within Victoria Peak? Or have all these people and governmental agencies simply fallen prey to a phony treasure tale? As of now there are no answers to these questions.

5

Jean Lafitte's Booty

*I wiped away the weeds and foam,
I fetched my sea-born treasures home...*

Ralph Waldo Emerson

When talking about pirates, there are at least three names which always create a special excitement among treasure hunters: Blackbeard, Captain Kidd, and Jean Lafitte. The last is perhaps the most mysterious of the three. Notorious and much talked about for over 175 years, the man is as elusive as his lost treasure. Legends and tales about his wealth—which, at the time he was alive, was rumored to be close to ten million dollars—place the site of his renowned treasure in hundreds of locations on the continent from Florida to Mexico.

Jean Lafitte arrived in New Orleans as Captain Lafitte of the French privateer *La Soeur Cherie*. Little has been learned about his life before that point. Five years from the day the French ship dropped anchor for repairs and provisions, Jean and his brother Pierre were the co-owners of a blacksmith shop which was to be merely a front for illegal operations.

On Barataria, now called Grand Terre Island, was a group of individuals—the first of many to mistakenly think they could outwit Lafitte and use him for their own purposes. These people of various nationalities had gathered on the island for the sole purpose of raiding ships in the Gulf of Mexico. Although the pirating was successful, they needed a market for the stolen goods. Jean Lafitte was a shrewd businessman who traveled in the fashionable social circles of the city. The pirates decided Lafitte could sell much of the pirated loot, so they employed him as their business representative. History has shown that Jean was only too glad to cooperate in this enterprise.

Jean Lafitte was indeed shrewd, as the pirates soon discovered. Not only did Lafitte become wealthy from his commission on black market activities, but slowly he began to take control of the independent pirates. Within a few years the pirates found themselves working for the man they had hoped to make work for them. Lafitte directed the operations of about six ships which sailed under the flag of the small South American nation of Cartagena, a country now part of Columbia. Cartagena had at this time just gained its independence from Spain and allied itself with Lafitte against its former mother country. Of course Spanish ships were the primary targets for pirating.

The market for the pirate treasure burgeoned, and the

stolen goods were funneled into New Orleans at an ever increasing rate. Law enforcement officials could do little to stop Lafitte's operations. First, the merchants of the city had numerous customers for the cheap merchandise among the wealthy plantation owners. Also, although the selling of these goods was against the United States revenue laws, the U.S. Government was unpopular in that area.

When the War of 1812 erupted, British agents contacted Lafitte because Barataria Bay was an important entry into New Orleans which the British hoped to capture. In return for his cooperation, the British promised to pardon Lafitte and give him $30,000 and a captaincy in the Royal Navy. Jean had previously served as a captain in France's forces under Napoleon, so this was not so outrageous an offer. Lafitte only pretended to join them; actually he was collecting all the information possible about a British attack on New Orleans. He then brought these secrets to U.S. officials along with the offer to have his band help the Americans. Not only did the military officials refuse, but they sent an armed ship to destroy the pirate stronghold on Barataria. The troops did capture some of Lafitte's ships, but they did not destroy the fortress, nor did they capture Lafitte.

Lafitte would not give up in his effort to assist the Americans. A second offer was made, this time to General Andrew Jackson, who accepted readily. The help of Jean Lafitte and his Baratarians was instrumental in the defeat of the British by American forces during the Battle of New Orleans. Lafitte emerged a national hero from the War of 1812. President James Madison issued full pardons to all the pirates with the understanding that they would no longer engage in illegal activities in the Gulf Coast area or in any other region of the country.

A life of legality was not for Lafitte, however. Soon he and his band were back on the high seas, seizing ships and smuggling the stolen goods into New Orleans. The law enforcement agencies mounted an attack against Barataria and drove Lafitte out of Louisiana. Before he left, however, Lafitte managed to collect and bring along his personal fortune. Reports indicate that Lafitte's next home was Padre Island, a crescent-shaped slice of land off the coast of Texas. Many a sea adventurer met his death on the sandy shores of Padre Island, because Lafitte and his men would set up lights on shore to confuse the sailors and lure their ships into shallow waters. The vessels would run aground, and Lafitte's band would steal the cargoes. From there Lafitte moved to the place now called Galveston Island but which Lafitte named Campeachy.

His life while on Campeachy has been source of many stories, books, and movies, but these accounts are mere speculation. As with most of his life and activities, Jean Lafitte hid behind a cloak of mystery. He constructed what was a combination home, warehouse, and fort. The stronghold was called Maison Rouge, and Lafitte ruled it and all of Campeachy like a medieval lord. The island became a center for pirates, adventurers, and about four hundred survivors from Napoleon's defeated armies. During this time Lafitte and his one thousand followers were a menace to any and all shipping on the Gulf of Mexico and the Caribbean Sea. Over a hundred Spanish ships alone were plundered, not to mention the ships of other flags which fell prey to Lafitte's ruthless pirating. He rapidly became the archenemy of the shipping trade.

Cries of outrage from American merchants finally prompted the U.S. Navy to send a warship to Campeachy. Though Lafitte tried to compromise by claiming his men would cease attacking American ships, he was not successful in dissuading the military force from evicting him. In 1820 Lafitte packed all his accumulated treasures into the *Pride* and, with a hand-picked crew, sailed away. Local stories say the pirates who stayed behind went on to start many of today's most influential families in Galveston. Certainly these men helped shape the city's history.

But what about Jean Lafitte?

Again, secrecy shrouds his life. Many people accept the story that he could not forsake piracy, so he continued his life of crime along the Yucatán coast. Nothing definite is known about his death either, but reportedly Jean Lafitte contracted fever and died in Mexico in 1826. Other historians have followed a different tack.

Did pirate Jean Lafitte become businessman Jean Lafitte who lived in St. Louis and did not die until 1854 in nearby Alton, Illinois? If so, had he retrieved portions of his own treasure to finance these business ventures? Since little was known about Lafitte before he appeared in New Orleans and even less is known about him after he was driven off Campeachy, these are difficult questions to answer.

If few facts exist about the man, what facts are available about his treasure?

Even less.

Most experts agree, however, that Lafitte would have

wasted no time in hiding his hoard either in one particular spot or scattered in several places. The seas were dangerous in those days, and his solitary ship would have been an attractive target for other pirates—particularly if they realized the *Pride* bore the total Lafitte wealth. There is reason to suspect the pirate buried his booty.

Possibly he returned to Padre Island. One of the most persistent rumors about Lafitte's treasure is that he imbedded the chests on Padre Island under a large millstone inscribed with the command, "Dig Deeper!"

Padre Island is visited by treasure seekers today, but not only in a quest for Lafitte's cache. Many ships from the 1500s onward have floundered and smashed on the island's shore. After a heavy storm at sea, people walk along the beaches, searching for old English and Spanish gold and silver coins which wash onto the sand. Other treasure hunters have found jewelry or packets of paper money in rusty cans on Padre Island. The wells which Lafitte and his followers built when they first used the island as a base of operations are now a tourist attraction, but his treasure, if it is there, still eludes the seekers.

Several years ago a group of searchers had obtained an old chart which indicated a spot where a spanish dagger plant and three brass spikes would lead them to the Lafitte treasure. They found thousands of spanish dagger plants but no brass spikes. They probably also discovered they had been sold a phony map. Bogus treasure maps are almost as plentiful as imaginative tales of buried treasure.

In all likelihood Lafitte would not have hidden his accumulated wealth on an island which had a reputation as being his former stronghold. Such a place would have been one of the first scoured by persons seeking that treasure. And he certainly would not have left a clue like a millstone with carved directions!

Other theories exist about Lafitte's fortune. There is speculation that over the years of his pirating he buried portions in different locations. Pecan Island, Louisiana, is a favorite hunting place. Pecan Island is not truly an island but a long ridge covered with oak trees which rises abruptly from the surrounding country. At the time Pecan Island was discovered about one hundred years ago, the area was covered with pecan trees. But something else was there, something that led people to believe the land may contain some of Lafitte's treasure. *The ground was thick with human bones.* Some people maintain that Pecan Island is where Lafitte had his victims murdered.

Though the likelihood of a pirate hiding a treasure in such a well-marked spot is slim, treasure seekers have worked on Pecan Island for years. In 1925 a treasure hunting party employed dynamite. The men nearly blew themselves and all of Pecan Island into pieces. And not a single gold coin was found.

But solid evidence of another Lafitte treasure has been discovered. Lafitte and his gang attacked a Spanish brig named *Santa Rosa* which carried a cargo of Mexican silver ingots worth two million dollars. The pirates transferred the silver to the *Pride* and sank the *Santa Rosa*. Later, in the summer of 1816, Lafitte decided to move the treasure from Maison Rouge on Campeachy to an inland hiding place. The Lafitte wagon train was to roll along the route called Trammel's Trace through the present towns of Carthage, Marshall, and Texarkana.

Early in the trip the men camped one night by Hendricks Lake near Galveston. Suddenly two hundred Spanish soldiers dispatched to recapture the silver surprised the men. Lafitte's band cut the mules loose and shoved the seven silver-laden wagons down the hill. Much to the dismay of the Spanish, the vehicles rolled into Hendricks Lake and disappeared beneath the water.

With both the pirates and the soldiers knowing the location of the sunken silver, it would be logical to suppose that *someone* had recovered the treasure. Yet in 1920 a party of fishermen brought up three silver bars from the lake bottom. Additional attempts to retrieve the ingots, if they are all still there, have failed. Some believers have even suggested draining the lake.

Perhaps the most authenticated story about Jean Lafitte deals with what happened to the *Pride* when the pirate captain left Campeachy for the last time. As the ship sailed around the sandy islands off Corpus Christi, a U.S. Navy gunboat took pursuit. Attempting to escape, Lafitte sailed up the Lavaca River. But as his vessel proceeded upriver it became hopelessly grounded on a sandbar. There was but one alternative. Quickly Lafitte ordered the treasure taken ashore and the ship scuttled.

The pirate crew trekked across the salt marshes. At one spot Lafitte had a pit dug and the treasure buried. He took a compass fix on the exact location and then, to mark the treasure, jammed a brass rod into the moist ground until only its tip could be seen.

Over the years many treasure hunters have tried their luck at finding this buried hoard. A certain Mr. J. C. Wise reportedly learned additional clues from two men who had been with Lafitte at the time the treasure was buried. Wise conducted numerous searches along the Lavaca River, but he was never able to find the spot where a brass rod protruded above the ground.

Years later a family named Hill purchased the property near the river mouth and used the grassy marshes as livestock pastures. One day a ranch hand rode through the area, searching for a stone or stump to use as a hitching post for his horse. As horse and rider moved through the thick grass, the man saw a brass rod sticking partially above the soil. He yanked the rod free and took the metal piece to the ranch when he returned later that day.

Several days later Hill saw the metal pole lying in the corral. When Hill, who knew the story of Lafitte's treasure, heard how the hired hand had discovered the rod, he asked to be taken to the spot immediately. Unfortunately, between the time of the discovery and the attempt to relocate the spot, a heavy rainstorm had hit that area of Texas. Time and nature had destroyed all telltale signs of the rod's original location. Although Hill made several subsequent intensive investigations of the region, he was never able to find the hidden treasure.

Does Lafitte's famous treasure still lie beneath the muddy salt marshes of the Lavaca River? Or did Jean Lafitte bury part of his pirated loot on the d'Estrehan plantation upriver from New Orleans? Some people insist the d'Estrehan family was extremely friendly with Lafitte and permitted him to use their property as a safe place for his wealth. Is the treasure in these two places or is it, as another story also postulates, in Galvez Town between New Orleans and Baton Rouge?

Many people claim to know the exact spot and even more wish they did, but at the moment Jean Lafitte's treasure is as much a mystery as the man himself.

6

The Burial Chamber of Kamehameha

Where is the man who owes nothing to the land in which he lives? Whatever that land may be, he owes to it the most precious thing possessed by man, the morality of his actions and the love of virtue.

Jean Jacques Rousseau

Each year on the eighth of May, Hawaii celebrates Kamehameha (Kah-*may*-ha-*may*-ha) Day, honoring the ruler who united the island chain under one government. A distinguished statue stands before the Judiciary Building in downtown Honolulu, draped with dozens of long, beautiful strands of flowers. The statue depicts a tall man, arms outstretched, wearing a feather helmet and cloak, holding a *pololu*, or a barbed spear, signifying peace. The legendary cloak of this king is part of the treasure story which began in 1782 when one of several Hawaiian kings died.

Three warring factions tried to obtain the dead man's empire which was on the island of Hawaii, now often called the Big Island. Kamehameha led one of these forces and was victorious. Then slowly he extended his power. First the island of Maui came under his control. In rapid succession more islands became his: Lanai, Molokai and then, in 1795, Oahu. Only Kauai and Niihau remained to be added to the empire. They were outlying islands, however, and could be taken at his leisure.

The period of Kamehameha's rule, 1795 to 1819, is about as close to a golden age as the islands ever came. The people had adapted well to living outdoors in the temperate climate and were now at peace. The islands were a true paradise. There were no mosquitoes, cockroaches, scorpions, rats, or diseases such as measles. All these were later introduced by the white man.

Once the civil wars ended in 1795, the king urged his people to return to farming and raise badly needed food. He himself set the example. Removing his royal garments, he donned the garb of a farmer and worked in the communal fields. This, as well as other achievements such as organizing the sandalwood industry which brought outside money into his nation, gave rise to a saying about Kamehameha.

"He is a farmer, a fisherman, a maker of cloth, a provider for the needy, and a father to the fatherless."

One of his judicial decisions is legendary. During the wars to unite the islands, Kamehameha personally led an attack on a group of unarmed fishermen. As he leaped from the war canoe into shallow water, his foot became caught in a crack in the lava. While Kamehameha was trapped, one of the fishermen struck him on the head with a canoe paddle which shattered. By the time the king's men had freed him from the lava crack, the fishermen had escaped.

Later the men were captured and brought before Kamehameha for punishment. Rather than seeking revenge, the king admitted that he was wrong in attacking unarmed men. He bestowed gifts upon the fishermen and set them free. He then proclaimed "The Law of the Splintered Paddle" which stated: "Let the aged men and women and little children lie down in safety in the road." From that time on, an attack on defenseless people was punishable by death.

Kamehameha was a statesman who knew how to retain the best of the old ways while adopting the best of the new. Even at the close of his life this king was making notable law. As he lay dying, the Hawaiian priests proposed to offer human sacrifices in an attempt to win the gods' favor and return their ruler to health. Kamehameha forbade the sacrifices and ordered that even during the period of mourning there would be no killings.

On May 8, 1819, Kamehameha the Great died in Kailua, Hawaii. As was the custom, the priests stripped the dead man's flesh from the bones and burned it in a temple fire. The bones were then wrapped in large leaves and gently placed in a woven basket of braided ie vines. After these rites which had, in the Hawaiians' belief, turned a dead king into an *aumakua,* or godlike ancestor, the trusted chiefs were given the honored task of hiding the bones of Kamehameha I from the world and its people.

The entire kingdom went into mourning. For two weeks people were forbidden to leave their homes even to fish or gather coconuts. If anyone was caught outdoors, that person would be put to death. Members of the *Alii,* or ruling class, followed tradition and either knocked out their own teeth or mutilated their flesh.

The end of the great leader is the beginning of the treasure story. Reportedly hidden along with the container bearing Kamehameha's bones were a portion of his personal wealth, rare Hawaiian artifacts, and his warrior robes. The cloaks were magnificent creations made from the feathers of two colorful and now-extinct birds. The tropical birds were forced into extinction by the demand for their feathers. One cape was made of five thousand tuft feathers of the o-o-a-a bird. The feathers from these robes alone would be worth a fortune.

The search for the burial chamber has brought some people to Kauai, the next island northwest of Oahu. The motivation for hunting there has to do with a now extinct tribe of people, small in stature, who supposedly lived there. The Hawaiians viewed them as a mysterious people. Possibly the chiefs thought this tribe could be entrusted to keep secret the location of the king's resting place. Another possible reason for picking Kauai is that the Na Pali coast is a very rugged, high-cliffed region with many deep ravines, making access difficult both from the land and the sea. Numerous caves can be found along the Na Pali coast. Kauai, however, would have been a lengthy trip from the Big Island where Kamehameha died.

The probability is greater that Kamehameha was buried on the island of Hawaii. This was his home island, his favorite place. Even after he had conquered all the islands in the chain, he insisted his capital should be on that island. But where on Hawaii would his bones have been placed?

Popular tradition has it that when the chiefs returned from the burial, they said, "Only the stars of the heavens know the resting place." Supposedly they placed the bones in a cave in the midst of a rain forest. There are several such sites on Hawaii. For example, stretches of rain forest can be found near Hilo.

The possibility exists that he was not buried in a cave but in a hand-dug underground chamber which many Hawaiians used as graves. Many of these can still be seen near Kamuela on the Big Island in open cactus fields. Most have caved in now. Searchers often disregard this type of site because these underground chambers were for the ordinary people. A man of Kamehameha's fame deserved something more special.

There is still another suggested burial site which, if it was used, is discouraging to archaeologists and treasure hunters alike. Some people think the king's remains and the other objects were thrown into a live volcano. There are several volcanoes on the Big Island not far from where Kamehameha died. The reasoning for this theory is that during his lifetime Kamehameha seemed favored by *Pele*, the volcano goddess.

In the first days of his thrust for power, Kamehameha had some minor skirmishes with Keoua, one of his enemies. When Keoua's armed warriors were returning to their base, they camped near the volcanic crater of Kilauea on Hawaii. While they were there, a terrible eruption began, filling the air with smoke, ashes, rocks, and poisonous gases. Although the men were safe in their camp, they divided into three groups and tried to return home. When the middle party was just beyond the crater mouth, a frightful explosion shook the ground. Four hundred people perished from burns and falling rocks, but mostly by suffocation. The event was hailed as an omen that Kamehameha had Pele on his side.

The next incident occurred in 1801 when one of the large craters atop Mount Hualalai in Kona erupted. The lava flow covered several villages, destroyed plantations, and filled up a deep bay along the coast. The priests tried unsuccessfully to stop the stream of molten rock by offering sacrifices. Kamehameha went to the river of lava. He too wanted to offer the goddess something to appease her anger. He cut off a lock of his hair and tossed it into the smoking lava. A day later the lava ceased to flow. Once again the people believed that Pele held a special affection for their king.

If the burial took place in a live volcano, then of course all the remains are lost forever. But other natural elements may have destroyed the bones, relics, and feather capes. Earthquakes are rather frequent on the islands. The cave or burial chamber may have collapsed. Periodic volcanic eruptions also strike the Big Island, the last major one being in 1975. The lava, which Kamehameha once was believed to be able to halt, may have buried the site.

Still the search goes on. Treasure hunters are urged to contact the State Archaeologist of the Department of Land and Natural Resources in Honolulu if they believe they have made a significant find. Contact should be made before anything is disturbed in the burial chamber. Priceless historical information might be lost if some treasure hunter acted too hastily in his or her search for wealth. By receiving advice from an archaeologist, the treasure seeker has nothing to lose —and the thanks of the Hawaiian people to gain.

7

Treasure Train: The Confederate Papers

> *It is ... unwise and unworthy of us ... to allow our energies to falter, our spirits to grow faint, or our efforts to become relaxed under reverses, however calamitous.*
>
> Jefferson Davis, April 4, 1865

The day of April 2, 1865, was bitterly deceptive in Richmond, Virginia. The sun was bright and the sky was beautiful. Daffodils bloomed in gardens, and throughout the city apricot trees were rich with blossoms, making the air fragrant. More importantly, no deep rumble of gunfire disturbed the stillness.

The city, however, was as dispirited as the rest of the Confederate States of America. Red flags dotted many Richmond houses, indicating people wanted to sell their homes and flee before the final downfall which seemed only days away. Military defeats of Confederate battalions had started coming at a frightening rate. Only Gen. Robert E. Lee provided a bulwark against complete Union victory.

All afternoon, wagons were backed up to the doors of various government department headquarters. Boxes of official documents were loaded aboard, and the wagons creaked to the railroad station. President Jefferson Davis had ordered the Confederate Government's capital moved to Greensboro, North Carolina.

What was left of the Confederate Treasury plus the private funds of the Richmond banks were also packed in bags and crates. The $500,000 in double-eagle gold pieces, silver bricks, gold ingots, and silver coins was to go on a special train guarded by sixty young midshipmen.

At the same time, President Jefferson Davis was readying his personal funds and private papers for a trip on the presidential train which would hopefully carry the government leaders away from the hands of the rapidly approaching Northerners. The plans specifically called for the treasure and the president's party to travel on different trains, so in case one was captured everything would not be lost.

Jefferson Davis and his cabinet arrived safely in Greensboro, North Carolina, but their stay was short. On the night of April 14, 1865, the same evening that President Abraham Lincoln was entering Ford's Theatre in Washington, D.C., to see a performance of *Our American Cousin,* a Confederate wagon caravan sneaked past enemy patrols under a sky ablaze from fires set by General Stoneman's advancing raiders.

Further south moved the two separate groups: Davis in a wagon train, the gold traveling by rail and wagon and then again by rail. South Carolina. Georgia. Finally as Jefferson Davis halted for a rest in Washington, Georgia, word came from nearby Abbeville that the treasure had arrived safely.

Fifty guards then transported the small iron chests, money belts, shot bags, and boxes to Washington, Georgia. President Davis ordered the $108,000 in silver coin to be split among the remaining Confederate troops as compensation for the back pay which they had never received. Each man was paid about thirty-two dollars.

Arrangements had been made to secretly bring Davis to a boat on the Indian River; he was to eventually reach Cuba or the Bahamas. Davis, however, refused to leave Confederate soil while a Confederate regiment was on it. He insisted that he would be able to reach Texas where a new Confederate government could be organized.

Before the party continued, more of the Confederate treasure was apportioned. The monies belonging to the Richmond banks, $230,000, were given to the proper agents in Washington, Georgia. The silver bullion, worth about $30,000, was stored in a local warehouse. Approximately $86,000 in gold was given to a naval officer who would take it to Charleston or Savannah concealed in the false bottom of a carriage. From one of these cities the gold would be shipped to a Confederate agent in Nassau, Bermuda, or Liverpool, England, for the Confederate Government's account.

The remaining $35,000, however, was destined to be known to treasure hunters as "The Confederate Treasure." This was packed aboard a wagon along with Davis's personal luggage consisting of a trunk and two chests. Several boxes of government papers were also stowed in the wagon. Capt. Micajah C. Clark was placed in charge of this wagon and had orders to move directly to Madison, Florida. Among Clark's eight selected guards was young Tench F. Tilghman who was a great-grandson of George Washington's noted aide-de-camp. Tilghman was entrusted to drive the wagon carrying the treasure and the personal papers of Davis.

At Sandersville, Georgia, the party split. Clark led the treasure train toward the appointed spot in Florida, and Davis turned southwest, hoping to find a safe route to Texas. The escort accompanying Davis was cheered by the fact they could now move much faster without the encumbrance of the treasure wagon. On the morning of May 10, however, a marauding party captured Jefferson Davis near Irwinville, Georgia.

The news of the Davis capture did not reach the treasure train immediately. The members of this caravan continued on for another week, dragging the two wagons through the muddy hills of Georgia. On May 15, they crossed the Withlacoochee River into the flatlands of Florida. Tilghman kept a diary which is the only account available about the events concerning the Confederate treasure.

On May 22, 1865, Tilghman wrote that the small group had camped "on the line of the Fernandina and Cedar Keys railroad in a forest northwest of Gainesville, near a large plantation." While encamped there the men learned of their leader's capture. Defeat now made their mission useless. Captain Clark distributed the money in the treasure wagon; each man receiving approximately $2,000. The group then dispersed. Before Tilghman left Gainesville, however, he buried his portion of the money plus the government archives and Jefferson Davis's personal papers.

The other men who accompanied Tilghman must have buried their share also, for when they traveled northeast to headquarters near Jacksonville, the party was searched and their revolvers confiscated at the time of their discharge. None of the treasure money was discovered during these searches. Nor does Tilghman's diary tell the location of the hidden money and the valuable documents.

An event occurred nearly two years later which seems to authenticate the fact that even today the Confederate treasure is still in the soil of Florida. In the spring of 1867, Tench Tilghman was at the Astor House in New York City, attending a convention of the Theta Delta Chi fraternity. He met a friend, William L. Stone, who was a fraternity brother. Stone reported that Tilghman told him that "with his own hands, he alone buried the treasure and the archives which had been entrusted to his care." Tilghman claimed that everything was still where he had hidden it.

Four days later Tilghman returned home and suffered a violent hemorrhage of his lungs. He died that night without revealing the treasure site. Therefore, unless in the period of time between speaking with Stone and the night of his death Tilghman returned to Florida, the treasure remains undisturbed. The possibility that Tilghman retrieved the treasure in those four days is highly unlikely.

Time has changed the meaning of the term *treasure* when people discuss the Confederate valuables. Originally people were interested in the money Tilghman and the other men hid. But today the documents of the Confederate Government as well as the personal papers and belongings of Jefferson Davis would have tremendous historical value if found. Though much has been written about the Civil War, there are gaps which these papers could fill. Historians, museums, and publishers would pay a great deal to possess the historical items.

The area near Gainesville is remarkably unchanged since the Confederates camped near the railroad line and the plantation. The region has escaped suburban sprawl, for only a few houses, stores, and service stations have been constructed. The plantation belonging to the Yulee family—Cottonwood—is gone, replaced by tall pines and huge water oak trees.

And the Confederate treasure beckons some resourceful hunter as it has for more than one hundred years.

8

Arizona's Lost Dutchman Mine

Gold! Gold! Gold! Gold!
Bright and yellow, hard and cold.

Thomas Hood

There are literally thousands of lost mines in the western section of the United States—mines of silver, gold, and turquoise to name several varieties. But none has captured the imaginations of both active seekers and armchair treasure hunters alike as much as the Lost Dutchman Mine. A conservative estimate of the number of people who have actively sought to locate the mine has been placed at 100,000. And thousands of claims have been filed in that section of the Tonto National Forest where people believe the lost mine exists. Newspaper and magazine articles galore as well as numerous books have been written about the mine.

Any serious attempt at reporting, however, generally

carries a genuine warning: be properly prepared to embark on a search or keep away from the area. The mine is located in the Superstition Mountains of Arizona, a rugged, hostile range in the Sonoran Desert about thirty-five miles east of Phoenix. The brooding, dangerous region seems determined to retain its secret, for many people have died in futile attempts to find the fabled riches. Arguments have erupted between mining partners with at least one person dead before the fight was over. Cliffs, rattlesnakes, and wandering lost in the wilderness have claimed other lives. Men have been murdered under strange circumstances with no clues ever found to explain their deaths. Seekers are therefore warned to enter with adequate protection and knowledgeable guides plus a thorough know-how about survival in a harsh, desolate area.

The region's ability to induce awe—and to be a setting for death—started with some of its earliest inhabitants. Archaeologists cannot pinpoint the time the Pima and the Maricopa Indians entered that part of Arizona, but the tribes were well established when the Apaches migrated there in the 1400s. The Pimas and Maricopas were frankly frightened of the Superstition Mountains and would not enter them under any circumstances.

Forced from Mexico by the Spanish conquerors, the Apaches came to Arizona already bearing a strong hatred for the Spanish. The Apaches were fierce warriors and did not share the other tribes' timid views about the mountains. They used the Superstition Mountains as a base of operations, swooping out of the hills on horseback to attack the more peaceable peoples and then hurrying back to the safety of the peaks where they would be safe from persuance.

One incident, however, was to change the Apaches' feelings toward the Superstitions and ultimately affect the history of the Lost Dutchman Mine.

The Maricopas had grown weary of the continual raids by the Apaches and decided to wage a fight to the death. They engineered a trap which caught the Apaches unawares. After the first skirmish which sent the Apaches racing for the Superstitions, the Maricopas followed, their fear of the mountains replaced by the deadly goal to exterminate the enemy. Once the Apaches were on home ground, however, the tide of battle swung the other way—and the Maricopas were defeated.

Though they had won, the Apaches suffered tremendous losses. In council the tribe decided that the mountains must be the home of the gods, spirits who had become angered because the Indians permitted the battle to take place there. Thus the Superstition Mountains became sacred to the Apaches, and death awaited those who would dare commit sacrilege.

In 1821 Mexico gained her independence from Spain. At that time Arizona and New Mexico became Mexican territory. But in 1846 border disputes with the United States produced a full-fledged war, and most of the area which would eventually become these two states was acquired by the United States from Mexico.

The story of the Lost Dutchman Mine begins with the Peraltas, a wealthy Mexican family reported to have been the original discoverers of the mine. But whether the Apaches were becoming too hostile or the United States was about to acquire that section of Arizona through the Gadsden Purchase, the Peraltas decided to extract one last load of gold and go back to Mexico.

The wagon train filled with smelted gold never left the Superstition Mountains. The party was surprised by the Apaches; only one boy escaped death. Some versions of the story claim that two brothers managed to survive and return to Mexico. The Indians followed a procedure that they had developed over the years when attacking other miners who tried to remove ore from their mountains. They buried the recaptured gold in pits or placed the gold in caves, thus in effect returning the ore to the home of its rightful owners —the gods.

At this point Jacob Walzer was waiting in the wings, about to walk onstage and become as controversial as the mine itself. Walzer, in some reports called Walz, was not really Dutch, despite the name given to his mine. He had been born in Germany and educated at the Heidelberg University. Following his formal education he worked for a number of years as a mining engineer in various countries. In 1862 he arrived in the port of New York City as an immigrant. Census records prove that Walzer was living in Prescott, Arizona, two years later. Perhaps the most distinguishing characteristic of the man was his snow-white beard. In 1938 a bronze plaque was erected at the foot of Superstition Mountain, stating, *"Here Lie The Remains Of Snowbeard The Dutchman."*

The above facts are authenticated by official records. But dispute rages about Jacob Walzer's personality. There are those who describe him as brash, cold-blooded, and greedy. Others say he was quiet, had only a few friends, and would never harm anyone except in self-defense. The legends about the mysterious man himself are as puzzling as those which try to explain how he first discovered the Lost Dutchman Mine.

One story says that Walzer and his partner, Jacob Wisner, were on a prospecting trip when they met another group which contained the lone survivor, then much older, of the Apache raid on the Peraltas. When Walzer and Wisner realized these people knew the whereabouts of a rich gold mine, they surreptitiously trailed them until the second party had reached their destination. Once the location was known, Walzer and his partner supposedly, in an act of detestible greed, murdered the other people and claimed the mine as their own.

This kind of tale makes for good storytelling around a campfire, and certainly incidents like that did occur, but there is a more reputable account of how Walzer found the mine. Remembering that Walzer was a trained mining engineer of many years experience, we can assume skill on his part.

Around 1870 Jacob Walzer and his partner entered the Superstitions on another prospecting trip. The previous ones had proven fruitless. And this one too was unsuccessful at first. Just as they were about to abandon their efforts, a trail led them to what seemed old mine workings. Assaying ore samples from this mine confirmed their hopes. The vein was an extremely rich one. They returned to Florence, Arizona, and used some of the gold to buy supplies necessary to begin full-scale operations. The citizens of the West at that time were ultrasensitive to any rumors of gold strikes. The use of gold to buy a large amount of goods was a highly suspicious action to the Westerners. Therefore little time passed before the townspeople were whispering about a possible strike in the Superstition Mountains.

A month later the duo reappeared in Florence with a much larger amount of gold and obtained even a greater amount of supplies. By the time they had departed from town, word had spread rapidly. Walzer and Wisner had made a hit. Somewhere in the Superstition Mountains the men had discovered a bonanza mine!

Walzer next arrived in town alone several months later, having left Wisner to work the mine alone. When the "Dutchman" returned to the Superstitions, he discovered Wisner's dead body lying half in the remains of the campfire, the victim of an Indian attack. Quickly Walzer buried his partner and then proceeded to camouflage the mine. A large stockpile of gold had been accumulated, so Walzer took as much as he could transport and carefully hid the rest. As the story goes, he then retreated from the Superstitions before the Apaches could eke out their revenge upon him as they had on Wisner.

The death of Jacob Wisner has given birth to a wide range of fanciful tales about his "true" demise. The most popular is the account which states that Walzer, inflamed with greed, realized all the gold could be his alone. One night he caught Wisner off guard and shot him. Walzer provided himself with an alibi by going through the pretense of entering town, telling people that Wisner was hard at work on the mine, and then later creating the lie about an Indian attack.

Persons who accept this legend cite the fact that Walzer buried the body in the mountains rather than bringing Wisner back to civilization as an attempt to hide the lie that Indians had killed the man.

For the next ten years, Walzer made occasional trips into the mountains. Whenever he returned he brought gold so pure that the ore could be shipped directly to a United States mint without being processed. On journeys to his mine, Jacob Walzer was well aware that people were trying to follow him and learn the mine's location. He worked out elaborate routes which twisted and curved back upon themselves so that individuals seeking to track him hopelessly lost the trail. Each time, Walzer would come back with enough gold to sustain his simple living habits for the next months or years. Records indicate that between 1880 and 1889 Jacob Walzer turned over to the government more than $250,000 in gold. *That* is no legend.

During his last years Walzer became a sort of "character" around Phoenix. If a person bought him a few drinks, Walzer would reward the individual with a single clue to the whereabouts of the Lost Dutchman Mine. Another fragment of the Walzer legend lingers on. This is about his death in 1892 following a lengthy illness. Supposedly he promised the old Indian woman who nursed him through those final days that he would leave her a map to the mine in his strongbox. The container was opened after Walzer's death. No map was there. Had the map been stolen—or was this merely another facet of the Walzer legend? Over the years the "authentic" Walzer map has appeared innumerable times, but these charts have always proved worthless.

And what about those verbal clues which Jacob Walzer so freely sprinkled through the bars of Phoenix? There are a surprising number of them; a few were often repeated by a man who appeared to take delight in riddles.

- One popular statement by Walzer was that no *miner* would ever find his mine. Did this mean that he had worked the mine out and was living on all the smelted gold? Or was he just proud of his clever feat of camouflaging the entrance so that no one *at all* could find it?

- Another hint seems to connect with this one. Walzer described the mine as a chimney formation which means a vertical shaft would have to be dug in order to obtain the ore. Walzer always added that the shaft was rose quartz and about eighteen inches wide. The gold, he said, would be found within this chimney formation. As most prospectors know, gold ore can be discovered in rose quartz. Was Walzer hinting, however, that the shaft was already dug and his mined gold was secreted inside the chimney formation, waiting just to be removed?

Both clues might also add up to another explanation of the Lost Dutchman Mine. As mentioned earlier, the Apaches attacked numerous miners and wagon trains bearing smelted gold. Had Walzer and Wisner actually found a cache hidden in a cave or shaft by the Indians who felt they were returning the stolen gold to their gods? Is this why no miner would find a mine?

Could the Lost Dutchman Mine not be a mine but a hidden deposit of previously dug and purified ore?

Jacob Walzer admitted other facts which relate to the mine's location. At first glance these clues seem to be direct step-by-step directions to follow to reach the mine.

• If an individual wants to find the mine, he or she must locate a deep canyon which runs north-south. The canyon will have the ruins of a stone house at the head. The old Military Trail in the Superstitions follows the bottom of this canyon and can be seen from the mine.

There are at least nine north-south canyons in the mountains. Only three, however, have the required ruins at the head. At the junction of three other canyons such ruins exist, but Walzer clearly stipulated the stone remains were at the head of the canyon.

• The mine is a cone-shaped pit which is in a ravine high on the side of a mountain. The mine's mouth faces west, but a person cannot spot the structure from below.

• The mine is situated in terrain so extremely rugged that a seeker has to be almost on top of it before he or she can see it.

Other clues which might seem to aid a searcher were released by Walzer. If so many exact details are available to the public, why have 100,000 people hunted for the mine and never found it?

There may be a number of reasons. Some searchers claim that each of Walzer's clues do fit a section of the Superstitions. But when a person puts them together, the telltale landmarks are scattered throughout the mountain range. Possibly Jacob Walzer was having fun in his senior years by purposely giving one prospector a clue which would lead him west, a second hunter a hint which would send him scurrying to the south. Another reasonable explanation why no one has found the lost mine may be that a severe earthquake rocked the Superstition Mountains in 1887. As far as anyone can tell, Walzer did not return to his mine after that quake. Many of the clues (if they were accurate) or even the mine itself may have been buried or smashed by the avalanches kicked off by the quake.

Earthquakes and inconsistent clues have not prevented searchers from combing the mountains since even before Walzer died in 1892. And stalking some of these hopeful searchers was tragedy.

In June, 1931, Mr. Adolph Ruth arrived in Apache Junction, Arizona, to search for the lost gold mine. Though the Superstitions already had a history of fatalities, the crippled government worker made two bad mistakes from the onset of his mission. First, he told everyone he encountered that he had in his possession an old Spanish map indicating the exact site of the Peralta-Walzer mine. Then, Ruth ventured into the mountains alone. Either course of action could be harmful; combined they were to be deadly.

Two local cowboys guided Ruth to a water hole in West Boulder Canyon. They helped the handicapped man set up camp and then returned to town. That was the last anyone saw Adolph Ruth alive. Six months later, his skull with a bullet in it was found on Black Top Mountain. A month later his body was found several miles away. What remained of his personal possessions was carefully searched, but no map could be found among his belongings. Local residents nodded knowingly: Greed was a strong passion, and Ruth had talked too much.

A strikingly similar case occurred sixteen years later in 1947 when James Cravey set out on a solitary search for the

Lost Dutchman Mine. Cravey hired a helicopter to pack him into the desolate Superstitions. The chopper deposited him near the head of La Barge Canyon. Cravey set up camp and waved a farewell to the aircraft pilot. James Cravey's body was found seven months later. His murder was almost identical to the Ruth killing.

This similarity in the deaths of the two men gave rise to wild rumors that an insane murderer was protecting the secret of the Lost Dutchman Mine. Though police investigations turned up no clues, many persons still believe that the theory was correct. Years have now gone by with no similar incidents, so certain individuals think that the area's insane killer has himself died.

From 1951 to 1961, twelve more people died and two additional persons disappeared without a trace in the Superstition Mountains. Of the twelve deaths, five were solved. This leaves seven people who have been shot and killed by unknown assailants.

There have been so many fatalities—homicidal and accidental—that the federal government is seriously considering closing the area to treasure hunters. Not only are some people injuring themselves because they have not taken the proper precautions, but there are even fanatics who are employing dynamite in their frenzied search, endangering the lives of themselves and others *plus* doing irreparable damage to the National Forest.

Whatever the government's decision, we can be certain that interest in the Lost Dutchman Mine will not wane. Recently a road construction crew was building a new highway near the Superstitions. The bulldozer unearthed a pit containing old digging tools, and work was halted while archaeologists investigated the relics. Meanwhile crowds gathered on the scene, certain that Jacob Walzer's mine had finally been discovered. Dating techniques showed the tools were of Spanish origin and dated back several hundred years before Jacob Walzer arrived in Arizona. Though in itself a wonderful, if accidental, historical find, this discovery frustrated many people.

Once again the lure of the Lost Dutchman Mine had attracted seekers—and once again disappointment was the result.

9

The Treasure of the Merida

> *And down in fathoms many went the captain and the crew ...*
>
> William Schwenck Gilbert

Stories about curses placed on treasures, or on those who seek these particular hoards, abound in the annals of treasure hunting. But there is a treasure, estimated to be worth more than five million dollars, which has the dubious honor of being one of the few caches *officially* cursed. And for those who scoff at such things, be aware that insanity, murder, and suicide are woven through the fabric of the treasure's history. In addition, the location of the treasure has long been known, yet no one has recovered anything other than a coin worth seven dollars.

The origin of much of these riches was the Temple of Aama in Burma where the wealth had been accumulating for centuries. A member of the Hapsburg family of Europe, Count Hermann, looted the temple, bringing the jewels and gold back to Austria. When the loss was discovered, the high priest of the temple went into meditation for a solid week. On the eighth day he rose at dawn and began to intone the curse. The number of inflictions this malediction placed upon those who had stolen the holy temple's treasure was so long, according to official records, that the priest did not finish his pronouncement until noon. There are those who say that all his ill wishes came true.

Count Hermann no sooner arrived back in Vienna, Austria, when his relatives, excited by the wealth, seized the treasure and had the count placed in a mental institution where, it is assumed, he died insane. The treasure found its way into the hands of another Hapsburg, Emperor Franz Josef of Austria-Hungary. The curse seemed to continue its work on the new owner of the jewels. Few rulers have had such an unhappy reign.

The House of Hapsburg began to self-destruct. Many members hated Franz Josef so much that they fled penniless rather than live under his domination. His queen, Elizabeth of Bavaria, was murdered by a shoemaker. The emperor's son Rudolf either killed himself or was murdered after he shot his sweetheart. Even though Franz Josef had by this time given away the cursed treasure, more disaster plagued his life.

His nephew Franz Ferdinand was assassinated at Sarajevo. The incident ignited the hidden enmities between the European countries and thus marked the beginning of World War I. This conflict saw the end of the Hapsburg rule and the defeat of Austria. And the seeds of hatred planted by World War I produced an even greater holocaust—World War II.

But long before these tragedies, the treasure had to cross the Atlantic Ocean.

While the United States was deep in a civil war, Napoleon III saw an opportunity to set up a puppet government in Mexico and establish a foothold for France in the Western Hemisphere. With a shipment of troops and a promise of huge loans, Napoleon placed Franz Josef's brother Archduke Maximillian as emperor of Mexico. As a gift to Maximillian and his wife Charlotte (who the Mexicans called Carlotta) Franz Josef gave the jewels and treasure which had been stolen from the Burmese temple. Generosity was not a characteristic of Franz Josef, so many persons claim the Austrian ruler had already realized that the curse on the treasure might well be a real thing.

The dreams of Napoleon as well as those of Maximillian and Carlotta were destined to be brief. In fact, you might say they were cursed from the beginning.

First, Napoleon's theory that the Civil War would divide America into two smaller, weaker nations did not prove accurate. Also, the Mexicans could not accept a foreigner as their ruler. Napoleon quickly recalled his troops to Europe. With the armed support gone, Maximillian was faced with uprisings.

Carlotta journeyed to Europe to visit the crowned heads, hoping someone would send troops to preserve Maximillian's power. While engaged in this task, she received word that Maximillian had been captured by Mexican revolutionaries and shot. Unable to accept the death of her husband and the loss of her throne, Carlotta retreated into her own world where she believed she was speaking to Maximillian, ruling Mexican affairs, and wearing her fabulous pearl and ruby necklace. Her father, King Leopold of Belgium, quietly locked her away in a castle where all her attendants continued the pretense until Carlotta, or Charlotte, died at the age of eighty-six.

Meanwhile the Burmese-Hapsburg jewels and gold remained in Mexico where ten years later they fell into the hands of President Porfiro Diaz. The leader was a president in name only, for he actually ruled as a dictator. For a while Mexico flourished under Diaz's control, but as the twentieth century dawned there were increasing numbers of riots and aborted revolutions. Knowing he would soon have to flee to Europe, Diaz chartered a steamer, the *Merida*, and had her fitted with special strong rooms. In these reinforced cabins he placed not only the cursed Hapsburg treasure but much of the gold and silver of the Mexican treasury. Diaz reached Paris safely; the jewels did not.

When the *Merida* steamed out of Veracruz harbor, she carried an impressive cargo. In one strong room was the $5,500,000 treasure of the Hapsburgs which included Carlotta's pearl and ruby necklace. In addition there were 827 silver bars valued at $237,500. In another strong room were the valuables of the passengers. Below deck the liner had a consignment of 699 bars of copper, mahogany logs, and 6,000 tons of Jamaican rum.

While the *Merida* was plowing through a dense fog off Cape Hatteras, North Carolina, she was sliced in two by the

Admiral Farragut bound for Port Antonio, Jamaica. All crew members and passengers from the sinking ship were quickly transferred to the *Admiral Farragut,* but there was no time to take any of the valuables in either of the strong rooms. The *Merida* sunk on May 11, 1911. The *Admiral Farragut* had itself sustained heavy damage, so it sailed directly to New York City to deliver the survivors and undergo repairs.

Almost immediately, attempts to salvage the treasures aboard the *Merida* were started. In the same year, Capt. Charles Williamson, a professional at salvage work, spent two months trying to locate the site of the ship. He had no success.

Soon after, a Wall Street-financed expedition employing a yacht and trawler hunted for the *Merida,* but the searchers could not find the hulk. Thirteen years later another company which included Drexel Biddle, the wealthy Philadelphia sportsman, sailed through outer Chesapeake Bay, hoping to get a fix on the sunken ship. For the first summer they could find nothing. Then, in the summer of 1925, they claimed to have discovered the vessel. Unfortunately a fierce storm arose, and when they returned a few days later their marker buoys had broken loose and drifted away. Discouraged, they abandoned their search.

In 1931 Capt. Harry L. Bowdoin discovered what he thought was the resting place of the steamer. His men cut into the sunken hull and brought up a big iron chest. But to their disappointment the chest was already opened and all the contents were long gone. And even more embarrassing to the captain was the fact that he was twenty miles away from where the *Merida* had disappeared below the waves.

In the early 1960s, Lt. Harry E. Rieseberg reported that

he had found the wrecked steamer at latitude 37° 20′ N, longitude 74° 47′ W. This spot is approximately forty-five miles off the Virginia Capes and the mouth of Chesapeake Bay. Donning diving gear, he descended 192 feet into murky water. Through the vision plate in his brass helmet, he saw the remains of the once-proud liner.

In *Treasure of the Buccaneer Sea,* he described the *Merida.* ". . . it seemed big and old and quite lonesome resting there in its watery sepulcher, enshrouded in its green coat of barnacles, shell and sea growth."

Lieutenant Rieseberg, a professional diver and treasure seeker, realized that a large amount of money would be needed to cut into the ship and retrieve the cursed treasure. At this point he has not undertaken the job—nor has anyone else.

Has the curse of a Burmese priest caused all the hardships which befell those connected with the holy temple's treasure? There are some people who laugh and call the idea ridiculous. But then there are some people who do not believe in lost treasures.

10

Jesse James: His Cache

Jesse James was a two-gun man...
In seven states he cut up dadoes.
He's gone with the buffler an' the desperadoes.

William Rose Benét

There is a popular song, "The Ballad of Jesse James," which attempts to depict the Western outlaw as a folk hero. Nothing could be farther from the truth. Jesse and his brother, Frank James, were cold-blooded killers and the leaders of a vicious gang of criminals with a record of twenty-two holdups of U.S. banks, trains, and stagecoaches. Their melodramatic exploits received much public attention and therefore excited some people's imaginations. But those who found the James Gang glamorous were individuals who were not robbed of their savings or their lives by the band.

This man, one of the most notorious of American outlaws, was born Jesse Woodson James in Clay County, Missouri, on September 5, 1847. By the age of fifteen Jesse had already hardened to such a degree that he was incapable of compassion toward others. He had also become a quick draw and a sharp marksman. Obviously James had all the makings of a thief and murderer.

At this young age he left home, joined William Quantrill's Raiders, and with them eagerly took part in the bloody civil warfare in Kansas and Missouri. Jesse had no philosophical beliefs about either the Northern or Southern viewpoints concerning slavery. He merely wanted to live the life of an outlaw—plundering and murdering. At the end of the Civil War, he surrendered along with Quantrill's other followers and briefly lived a quiet existence. The life of a law-abiding citizen was not for Jesse James, however.

In 1866 he and Frank organized a band which included Bud Dalton and Cole Younger along with seven other cutthroats. These eleven men cut a swath through what are now the states of Missouri, Oklahoma, and Texas, robbing and killing. There were rewards posted for their capture throughout the West. The state of Missouri alone offered $10,000 for the capture of Jesse and Frank, dead or alive. The take from the gang's crimes has been estimated at close to $400,000. The ill-gained profits were split among the members; some buried the items for future use, while others spent their shares in a free-wheeling lifestyle.

In February 1876, however, the band executed a massive crime. They had traveled across the Mexican border a few miles from El Paso, Texas. There they ambushed a packtrain of twenty burros carrying two million dollars in gold bars belonging to a Mexican insurgent general. The outlaws killed the guards and drovers and led the loaded burros back into the United States. On March 1, 1876, they entered Indian territory and, on the fourth day of the month, camped in the Wichita Mountains of what is now south central Oklahoma. The site was located on Cache Creek which is south of the present town of Cement.

A hard decision faced the gang. What was to be done with the loot? If they continued bringing the burro train back to Missouri, their progress would be slow and the pursuing law enforcement officers would soon overtake them. Plus, having a group of branded burros with them would quickly attract attention. Jesse proposed that they bury the treasure. However, the gang members basically distrusted each other; the men argued, thinking that the James brothers would secretly return on their own and take all the gold for themselves. Cole Younger insisted that James give them proof that everyone would share equally when the time came to divide the wealth.

According to one account, Jesse then scratched a rough kind of contract on a brass bucket with a nail. He added the names of each gang member to this business deal. Appeased, the men began the task of hiding the two million dollars worth of bullion as well as the take from a former holdup.

The location was to be a small arroyo with a lone cottonwood tree growing there. The riches were deposited in a deep hole which was then refilled and camouflaged with boulders. The brass pail was supposedly buried near the treasure. For an additional marker, Jesse had a shoe removed from a burro and hammered into the base of the cottonwood tree. All the empty packs were unloaded from the animals and burned.

The burros were then turned loose in the mountains.

The same year which had seen a tremendous illegal haul also saw the beginning of the James Gang's downfall. After killing two people but failing to obtain any money in a Northfield, Minnesota, bank robbery, the band lost several of its members. Cole Younger, one of the gang's most trusted followers and effective criminals, was caught and sentenced to twenty-five years in prison. Jesse and Frank escaped, however, and went about the task of replacing the captured members. A fatal decision was made when Jesse decided to enlist two brothers, Robert and Charles Ford, to fill out the ranks of his band of thieves and killers.

The gang was relatively quiet for the next few years, but in 1879 they staged an attack on another train. At this time Governor Thomas T. Crittenden of Missouri had a huge reward posted for the James brothers. The money was destined to tempt one gang member.

Jesse was now living under the assumed name of Thomas Howard in St. Joseph, Missouri. There was a private joke among the gang that Jesse was deliberately using the governor's first name as his own. The joke, however, was not to end in a big laugh. On April 3, 1882, Bob Ford visited Jesse's home. Ford entered the house posing as a friend, but he left as an assassin. Catching Jesse unaware, Ford shot and killed the thirty-four-year-old outlaw leader. He then claimed the $10,000 prize. Thus the man, who from the age of fifteen had mercilessly employed a gun to steal and murder, himself died from a gunshot wound.

Following the death of his brother, Frank James surrendered to the authorities but was twice acquitted. In 1907 a 160-acre farm a few miles north of Fletcher, [wh]ere he settled down to become what appeared [ ] as an average citizen, farming and living with his wife, Ann. Frank James, however, had other reasons for selecting the Fletcher farm as his new home. The time had come to retrieve the Mexican gold.

But time had also become an enemy. In the intervening thirty-three years, the area had changed drastically. The land rushes and resultant homesteading in the state had destroyed all the familiar landmarks. Frank searched alone for a while and then was joined by Cole Younger when the latter was released from prison. But neither the brother of Jesse James nor the individual who had insisted on a contract promising an equal share of the gold could find the treasure site. When Frank James died in 1915 at the age of seventy-two, Cole Younger abandoned his search without ever reclaiming the burro-shoe treasure.

The searches of James and Younger, however, had attracted the attention of local residents. Stories had spread during those years, and people openly speculated about the suspicious actions of the two men. Three neighbors of Frank James—Addams, Pierson, and Doctor Wilbur Knee—ferreted out what information they could about the missing gold. They learned of the burro shoe plus two pick heads which were supposed to point out the direction to the treasure. The three men decided to try their luck at finding the raiders' loot.

A few miles from Cement they did find the bleached bones of an animal which they theorized might have been one of the burros freed by the James Gang in 1876. This was skimpy evidence in an area where many animals such as horses or cattle had died. Yet the gold seekers were encouraged. On they went until they eventually discovered a small, rocky arroyo which contained the decaying stump of a single cottonwood tree. Near the base of this once-living marker the men spotted a burro shoe. Elated, they began digging pits throughout the gulley. Their time and perspiration were wasted, though. The secret location eluded them, and in the end they had to admit defeat.

Their treasure-hunting expeditions, however, alerted many persons to the site. The area had become widely known as the location of a vast gold hoard buried by the James brothers. Other gold hunters tried to uncover the outlaw loot, but they too failed. Soon the story became a local legend, and, like a tale, subsequently fostered doubts concerning its authenticity. One man, however, was certain the treasure did exist.

In 1931 Deputy Sheriff Joseph Hunter of Rush Springs, Oklahoma, decided to try his luck. Returning to the now famous arroyo, Hunter searched the area methodically rather than digging haphazardly. After a few weeks of careful investigation, Hunter found an old, short-handled prospector's pick and the soot-covered frames of a number of packsaddles. The discovery of the burned remains of the burros' packs certainly seemed to indicate that he was in the area where the James Gang had unloaded the burros and thereafter burned the packs. Possibly the old pick had been used to dig the pit, or the tool might have been part of the clue which, as Frank James had said, was made up of two pick heads pointing the direction to the treasure.

About a month later Hunter unearthed a large, iron teakettle about fifty yards from the rotted stump. He worked the rusted lid off the container and dumped the contents onto a blanket.

Hunter stood there gaping at the small treasure. There were gold coins amounting in worth to about $5,000. Two other coins—a five-franc French coin dated 1811, and an 1841 large U.S. penny—were in the kettle. Hunter also found a gold and silver pocket watch. The watch case had the name Theodore Studley engraved in old German script. The timekeeping device had been manufactured by the New York Watch Company of Springfield, Massachusetts. Completing the find were two pearl brooches and a gold locket containing a ruby.

There are two theories related to this cache. Hunter figured the James brothers may have hidden the collection separately as a secret, personal share. Other people think the kettle contained the loot from the former robbery which was buried along with the Mexican gold. However the treasure had come to be placed there, Hunter was certain he was on the right track. Devoting as much time and work as possible, he continued his search for two more years. He then found another confirming clue: a brass pail with letters scratched on the outside surface. He could read part of the writing: *"On this 5 day of March, 1876 . . ."*

Hunter knew that the James Gang had reportedly been in the area those first few days of March, 1876, and realized that this pail held the solid contract which Cole Younger insisted be drawn up before the gold was buried. The brass bucket bore additional markings and inscriptions. The other writing was illegible, but the drawings appeared to be a grave, a cross, a burro and its pack, and, most importantly, an etched burro's shoe with an arrow pointing away from that telltale marker.

But what did these markings mean? Were the drawings a rough map composed of coded clues? If so, their meaning was too obscure.

Though the man continued his meticulous search of the territory, he never found the main body of the treasure. In 1948 he was interviewed for a newspaper article. He informed the reporter, "I'm going to find that two million bucks worth of gold bullion before I kick the bucket."

But time once again proved to be on the side of the hidden treasure. Deputy Sheriff Joseph Hunter died in 1953, the gold escaping him.

Though the burro-shoe treasure still has not been found, other Jesse James caches may have been located. In 1938 Mr. Floyd Terril, a professional treasure hunter, unearthed a James hoard near Chickasha, Oklahoma. The bandit loot, worth $38,650, was mostly made up of gold coins.

The hidden sites of still other James Gang gains are mysteries, but there is one treasure-hunting incident which is in itself strange. The event occurred in Arkansas and centers around a stone. A treasure seeker discovered this rock someplace between Plainview and Hot Springs, Arkansas. The stone bore a chiseled inscription: *"Frank–Jesse James. $32,000. 1877."* The rock had coded drawings which resembled those on Hunter's brass pail. The markings seemed to be a crudely-drawn knife, a three-pronged fork, and a cross. The last symbol was the one most similar to the shape etched on the brass bucket.

The finder told reporters and curious people that he

never located the treasure which, as this marker supposedly indicated, was buried somewhere nearby. He described in minute detail his fruitless, frustrating search and his final despair.

The townspeople, however, noticed the treasure hunter suddenly displayed an affluence not shown before. The Internal Revenue Service (IRS)—to which a tax on any found treasures must be paid—began making inquiries about the man's financial standing. Then, abruptly, in the midst of intensifying federal investigations, the man disappeared from his Hot Springs home. Though the IRS will neither confirm nor deny the fact, the rumor persists that their agents are hot on his trail.

But where is the burro-shoe treasure to which a trail of clues appears to lead?

Seekers have found the arroyo, the rotted cottonwood stump, the brass bucket bearing the contract, as well as the burros' charred packsaddles. All that seems to be missing is the two-million-dollar cache! Did some members of the outlaw band return and gather their hoard without informing the others? If so, Frank James and Cole Younger would seem like the people who ought to have known this and would not have conducted their own search.

In all probability, the gold is still in the deep pit where it was placed more than one hundred years ago. Time, which has defeated so many seekers, may turn out now to be an ally to some fortunate treasure searcher. Each year more sophisticated metal locating devices are being developed. As of now there is a relatively low-priced metal detector which will signal the location of a large body of metal sixteen feet below the surface of the ground. The next few years may see even more sensitive instruments becoming available to the average citizen. Not only may time provide the necessary equipment, but the use of such electronic devices will save time. No longer will a treasure hunter have to spend months or years digging throughout the arroyo. He or she may be able to pinpoint the gold's site before the first shovelful of dirt.

That lucky person may even turn out to be you!

Dig Deeper!

> *Over the mountains*
> *Of the Moon,*
> *Down the Valley of the Shadow,*
> *Ride, boldly ride, . . .*
> *If you seek for Eldorado.*
>
> Edgar Allan Poe

For those of us who do believe in lost treasures—at least in the treasure tales backed up by authenticated information—the search can be fun whether you are an armchair treasure hunter or one who actively works in the field.

Lost treasure stories exist not only in America but all over the world. True of too many is the fact that the caches are simply imagination. Therefore if you do embark upon a search, be sure to investigate all sources of information before you set out. The time will be well spent because you may unearth a single clue other people have missed.

Those individuals living in New York and Vermont may want to search for General Burgoyne's silver, lost or hidden during the Revolutionary War's Battle of Saratoga. For the persons living in the western section of the United States, robbers' loot such as that belonging to Butch Cassidy may literally be in your own backyard. And, of course, only fragments of Captain Kidd's pirate treasure have been found to this day.

The facts behind *these* treasures? Those stories will have to wait for another day.

Index

Able, Maj. Kenneth, 55
Admiral Farragut, 105
Apache Indians, 47, 88–90, 92, 94
Arizona, 88–91, 96
Arkansas, 49, 116
Aztec Indians, 19–24, 28

Banks, George, 13–5
Barataria, 60–62
Battle of New Orleans, 61
Beckwith, Marvin, 50
Berclett, Tom, 51–2
Bertrand, 15–6
Boggs, Liburn, 53
Bowdoin, Capt. Harry L., 105

Cache Creek, Oklahoma, 111
Campeachy, 62–3, 65–6
Carlotta, wife of Maximillian, 103–4
Cartagena, 60
Clark, Micajah C., 81–2
Confederate Government, 80–1, 83
Confederate Treasure, 80–2
Corbino, Sam, 15–6
Cortés, Hernando, 20–22, 28
Cravey, James, 96–7
Crittenden, Gov. Thomas T., 112
Crystal, Freddy, 25–8
Cuitlahuac, 22

Dalton, Bud, 110
Davis, Jefferson, 80–2
d'Estrehan plantation, 67
Diaz, President Porfiro, 104

Fiege, Capt. Leonard, 51–3
Florida, treasure site in, 82–3
Ford, Robert, 112
Ford, Charles, 112

Gaddis Mining Company, 54
Galveston Island. *See* Campeachy
Galveston, Texas, 63, 66
Gasiewicz, Lt. Col. Sigmund I., 52
Georgia, 80–82
Gold bars, 46–9, 52, 56, 110–1
Gold coin, 14–5, 41, 64, 115–6
Grand Terre Island. *See* Barataria

Hawaii, island of, 74–5
Hawaii, state of, 71, 74–6
Hendricks Lake, Texas, 66
Hill property in Texas, 67
Hopi Indians, 23
Howard, Thomas. *See* James, Jesse
Hunter, Deputy Sheriff Jos., 114–6

Inca Indians, 39

Jackson, General Andrew, 61
James, Frank, 109–14, 117
James, Jesse Woodson, 109–112, 114
Johnson Canyon, Utah, 25–6
Josef, Emperor Franz, 102–3

kiva, 23–4, 28
Kamehameha, 71–6
Kanab, Utah, 25, 27–8
Keoua, 75

Lafitte, Captain Jean, 59–68
La Rue, Padre, 46–7, 54
La Soeur Cherie, 59
Lavaca River, 66–7
Lee, General Robert E., 79
Lost Dutchman, 87–9, 93–4, 97–8
Louisiana, 62, 65, 68

Madison, James, 61
Mahone Bay, Nova Scotia, 31–2
Maison Rouge, 62, 65
Maricopa Indians, 88–9
Maximillian, 49, 103–4
McGinnis, Daniel, 31–3, 36, 40
Merida, 104–6
Mexico, 26–7, 46, 88, 103
Missouri, 109–12
Missouri River, 15
Montezuma, 20–2, 28
Montezuma's treasure, 22–5, 27–8

Nebraska, state of, 15
New Mexico, Museum of, 53
New Mexico, 23–5, 45–9, 53–5, 89
New Orleans, 59, 61–3, 67–8
New York, Saratoga, 119
Noble, Curtis, 50
North Carolina, 80, 104
Noss, "Doc" Milton, 47–51, 54, 56
Noss, Ova, 48–51
Nova Scotia, 31–2

Oak Island, Nova Scotia, 31–42
Oklahoma, 110–1, 113–4

Peralta family of Mexico, 89–91
Pima Indians, 88
Pizarro, Francisco, 39
Pride, 64–6
Pueblo Indians, 23–4
Pursell, Jess, 15–6

Quantrill, William, 110
Quetzalcoatl, 20–1

Restall, Robert, 37
Rieseberg, Lt. Harry E., 105–6
Robinson, Oscar, 25–6
Ruth, Adolph, 96
Ryan, Charles, 49–50

Santa Rosa, 65
Shinkle, Maj. Gen. John G., 54
Smith, John, 32–3
Smith's Cove, Nova Scotia, 36, 40
Stone, William L., 83
Sunken treasures, 15–6, 105
Superstition Mountains, 88–92, 95–7

Terril, Floyd, 116
Texas, coast of, 62, 64, 66
Texas, state of, 110
Tenochtitlán, 19–23
Tilghman, Tench F., 81–3
Tonto National Forest, 87
Trammel's Trace, Texas, 65–6
Triton Alliance, 37, 41–2

U.S. Dept. of Defense, 45, 51, 53–4
U.S. Treasury Dept., 45, 54
Utah, 25–8

Vaughan, Anthony, 32–3, 35
Victoria Peak, 45–7, 50–1, 53–6
Virginia, Richmond, 79

Walzer, Jacob, 90–8
War of 1812, 61
Washington, state of, 13
Williamson, Capt. Charles, 105
Wisner, Jacob, 91–3

Younger, Cole, 110–3, 115, 117

PRINTED IN U.S.A.

j973 Copy 1
MAD
Madison, Arnold
Lost treasures of America

DEC 15 '80
MAR 1 1983
JUL 9 1986
AUG 30 '90

Thompson Public Library
Thompson, Conn.

NOV 8 0

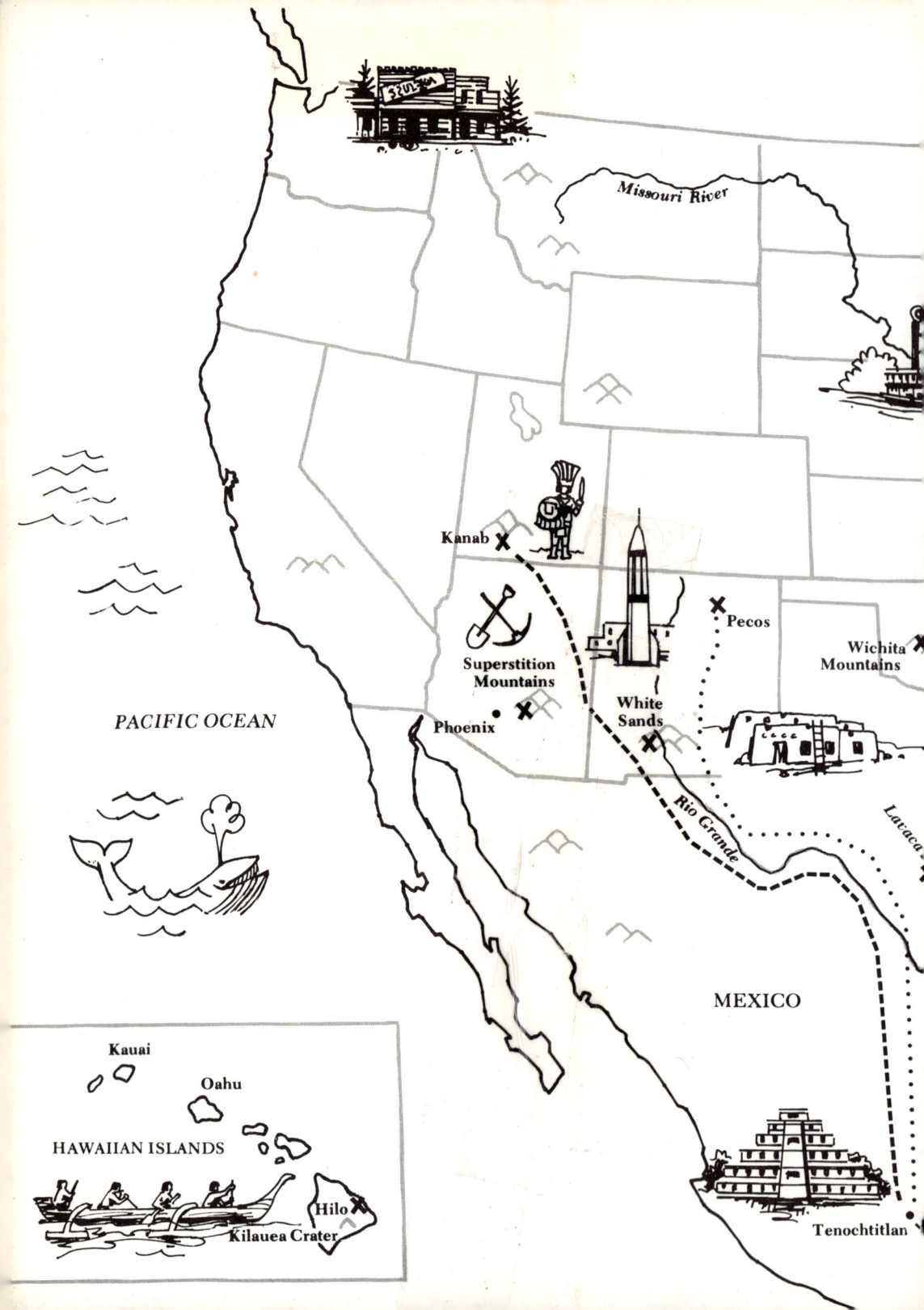